SCRABBLE®

CROSSWORD GAME

Score & Tile

T₁ R₁ A₁ C₃ K₅ E₁ R₁

STERLING

New York / London

www.sterlingpublishing.com

STERLING and the distinctive Sterling logo are registered
trademarks of Sterling Publishing Co., Inc.

Library of Congress Cataloging-in-Publication Data available

10   9   8   7   6   5   4   3   2   1

Word lists courtesy of *Scrabble®Wordbook* © 2007 by Mike Baron,
Sterling Publishing Co., Inc.

Word lists are based on *The Official Scrabble® Players Dictionary, Fourth
Edition*, Merriam-Webster, Inc.

Two-player scoresheet based on designs by Kate Fukawa-Connelly
and Steve Pellinen.

Published in 2007 by Sterling Publishing Co., Inc.
387 Park Avenue South, New York, NY 10016

Copyright © 2007 Hasbro.

Distributed in Canada by Sterling Publishing
c/o Canadian Manda Group, 165 Dufferin Street
Toronto, Ontario, Canada M6K 3H6

Distributed in the United Kingdom
by GMC Distribution Services
Castle Place, 166 High Street, Lewes,
East Sussex, England BN7 1XU

Distributed in Australia by Capricorn Link (Australia) Pty. Ltd.
P.O. Box 704, Windsor, NSW 2756, Australia

Sterling ISBN-13: 978-1-4027-5099-1
           ISBN-10: 1-4027-5099-4

For information about custom editions, special sales, premium
and corporate purchases, please contact Sterling Special Sales
Department at 800-805-5489 or specialsales@sterlingpub.com.

How to Use This Book

USING SCRABBLE® scoresheets is easy. For the two-player game, tear out the sheet from that section. If you don't want to flip the sheet over during play, tear out two pages and tape them together with the two different sides face up. Then you'll have a double-sided scoresheet that can be used for two games. You can record the tiles in your rack in the red boxes on the scoresheet and record the words you played in the remaining area of the box. The scores go to the left or right of the numbers; the score for that turn goes in the top half of the box, the running total just below it. On the back is a board for recording the plays and keeping track of the tiles.

If you're playing with three or four people, go to that section of the book, tear out a scoresheet, and write the players' names at the top of each column. The first score goes next to 1. The next score goes on the line with the "+" to the right of the 2, and the new total goes on the line below that. Continue this way until the end of the game. The "Tiles + or −" line is where the tiles at the end of the game go when someone goes out. On the back of the sheet, you can record your board and keep track of the tiles that have been played.

At the end of the book you'll find several useful lists that every player should try to commit to memory.

Good luck and have fun!

Date _____ Round 1 2 3 4 5 6 7 8 9 10 11 12 _____

Location _____

Rating	P1			P2		Rating
			1			
			2			
			3			
			4			
			5			
			6			
			7			
			8			
			9			
			10			
			11			
			12			
			13			
			14			
			15			
			16			
			17			
			18			
			19			
			20			
Tiles + or −				Tiles + or −		
Overtime Penalty				Overtime Penalty		
Final Score				**Final Score**		

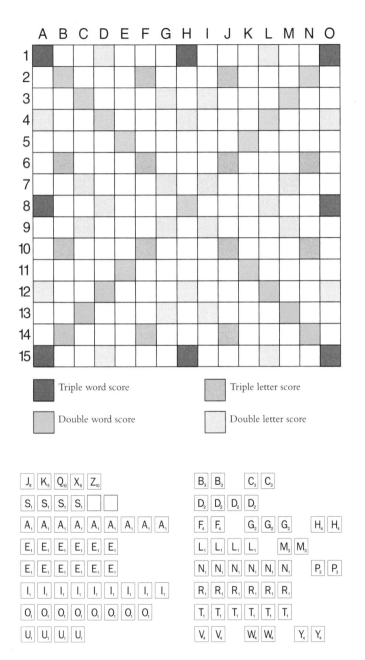

Date _____ Round 1 2 3 4 5 6 7 8 9 10 11 12 _____
Location _____

Rating	P1				P2		Rating
▭▭▭▭▭▭			**1**		▭▭▭▭▭▭	
▭▭▭▭▭▭			**2**		▭▭▭▭▭▭	
▭▭▭▭▭▭			**3**		▭▭▭▭▭▭	
▭▭▭▭▭▭			**4**		▭▭▭▭▭▭	
▭▭▭▭▭▭			**5**		▭▭▭▭▭▭	
▭▭▭▭▭▭			**6**		▭▭▭▭▭▭	
▭▭▭▭▭▭			**7**		▭▭▭▭▭▭	
▭▭▭▭▭▭			**8**		▭▭▭▭▭▭	
▭▭▭▭▭▭			**9**		▭▭▭▭▭▭	
▭▭▭▭▭▭			**10**		▭▭▭▭▭▭	
▭▭▭▭▭▭			**11**		▭▭▭▭▭▭	
▭▭▭▭▭▭			**12**		▭▭▭▭▭▭	
▭▭▭▭▭▭			**13**		▭▭▭▭▭▭	
▭▭▭▭▭▭			**14**		▭▭▭▭▭▭	
▭▭▭▭▭▭			**15**		▭▭▭▭▭▭	
▭▭▭▭▭▭			**16**		▭▭▭▭▭▭	
▭▭▭▭▭▭			**17**		▭▭▭▭▭▭	
▭▭▭▭▭▭			**18**		▭▭▭▭▭▭	
▭▭▭▭▭▭			**19**		▭▭▭▭▭▭	
▭▭▭▭▭▭			**20**		▭▭▭▭▭▭	
Tiles + or −					Tiles + or −	
Overtime Penalty					Overtime Penalty	
Final Score					**Final Score**	

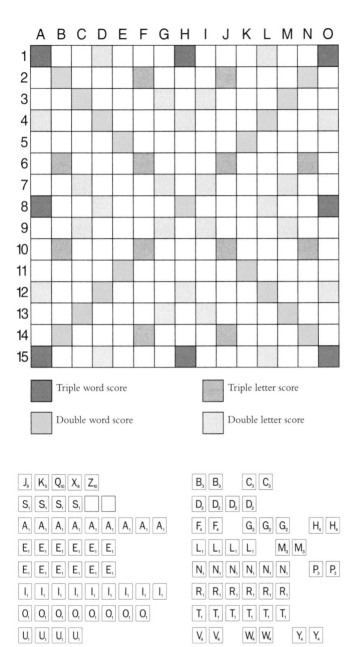

Date _____ Round 1 2 3 4 5 6 7 8 9 10 11 12 _____
Location _____

Rating	P1			P2		Rating
			1			
			2			
			3			
			4			
			5			
			6			
			7			
			8			
			9			
			10			
			11			
			12			
			13			
			14			
			15			
			16			
			17			
			18			
			19			
			20			
Tiles + or −					Tiles + or −	
Overtime Penalty					Overtime Penalty	
Final Score					**Final Score**	

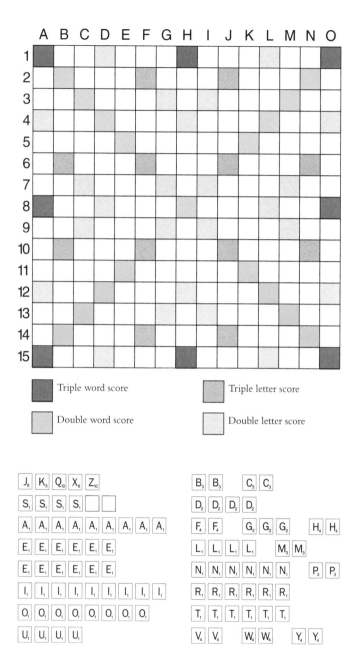

Date _____ Round 1 2 3 4 5 6 7 8 9 10 11 12 _____

Location _____

Rating	P1				P2		Rating
			1				
			2				
			3				
			4				
			5				
			6				
			7				
			8				
			9				
			10				
			11				
			12				
			13				
			14				
			15				
			16				
			17				
			18				
			19				
			20				
Tiles + or −					Tiles + or −		
Overtime Penalty					Overtime Penalty		
Final Score					**Final Score**		

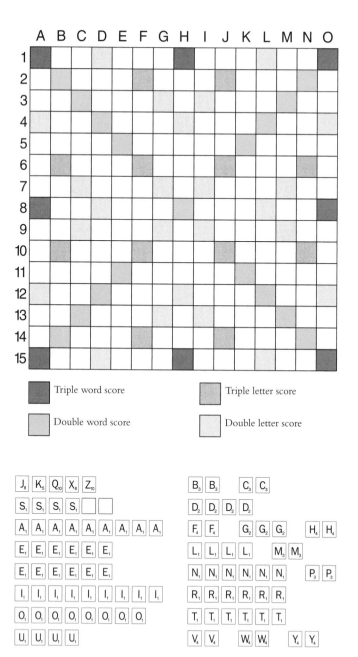

Date _____ Round 1 2 3 4 5 6 7 8 9 10 11 12 _____
Location _____

Rating	P1			P2		Rating
			1			
			2			
			3			
			4			
			5			
			6			
			7			
			8			
			9			
			10			
			11			
			12			
			13			
			14			
			15			
			16			
			17			
			18			
			19			
			20			
Tiles + or −				Tiles + or −		
Overtime Penalty				Overtime Penalty		
Final Score				**Final Score**		

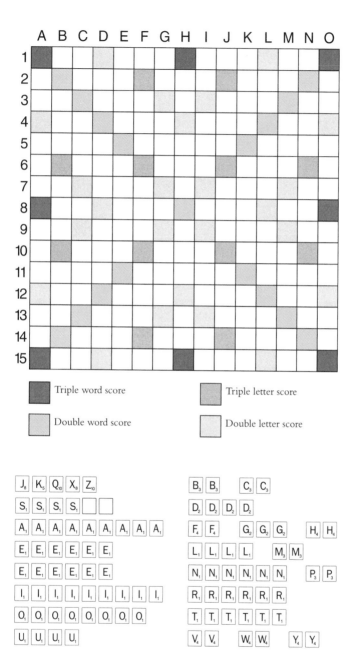

Date _____ Round 1 2 3 4 5 6 7 8 9 10 11 12 _____

Location _____

Rating	P1			P2		Rating
▭▭▭▭▭			**1**		▭▭▭▭▭	
▭▭▭▭▭			**2**		▭▭▭▭▭	
▭▭▭▭▭			**3**		▭▭▭▭▭	
▭▭▭▭▭			**4**		▭▭▭▭▭	
▭▭▭▭▭			**5**		▭▭▭▭▭	
▭▭▭▭▭			**6**		▭▭▭▭▭	
▭▭▭▭▭			**7**		▭▭▭▭▭	
▭▭▭▭▭			**8**		▭▭▭▭▭	
▭▭▭▭▭			**9**		▭▭▭▭▭	
▭▭▭▭▭			**10**		▭▭▭▭▭	
▭▭▭▭▭			**11**		▭▭▭▭▭	
▭▭▭▭▭			**12**		▭▭▭▭▭	
▭▭▭▭▭			**13**		▭▭▭▭▭	
▭▭▭▭▭			**14**		▭▭▭▭▭	
▭▭▭▭▭			**15**		▭▭▭▭▭	
▭▭▭▭▭			**16**		▭▭▭▭▭	
▭▭▭▭▭			**17**		▭▭▭▭▭	
▭▭▭▭▭			**18**		▭▭▭▭▭	
▭▭▭▭▭			**19**		▭▭▭▭▭	
▭▭▭▭▭			**20**		▭▭▭▭▭	
Tiles + or −					Tiles + or −	
Overtime Penalty					Overtime Penalty	
Final Score					**Final Score**	

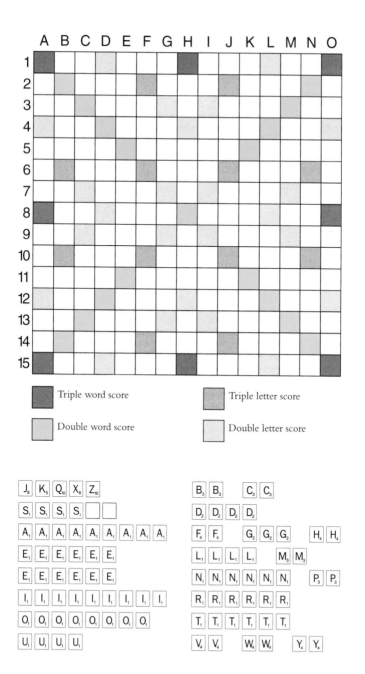

Date _____ Round 1 2 3 4 5 6 7 8 9 10 11 12 _____
Location _____

Rating	P1			P2		Rating
▭▭▭▭▭▭			1		▭▭▭▭▭▭	
▭▭▭▭▭▭			2		▭▭▭▭▭▭	
▭▭▭▭▭▭			3		▭▭▭▭▭▭	
▭▭▭▭▭▭			4		▭▭▭▭▭▭	
▭▭▭▭▭▭			5		▭▭▭▭▭▭	
▭▭▭▭▭▭			6		▭▭▭▭▭▭	
▭▭▭▭▭▭			7		▭▭▭▭▭▭	
▭▭▭▭▭▭			8		▭▭▭▭▭▭	
▭▭▭▭▭▭			9		▭▭▭▭▭▭	
▭▭▭▭▭▭			10		▭▭▭▭▭▭	
▭▭▭▭▭▭			11		▭▭▭▭▭▭	
▭▭▭▭▭▭			12		▭▭▭▭▭▭	
▭▭▭▭▭▭			13		▭▭▭▭▭▭	
▭▭▭▭▭▭			14		▭▭▭▭▭▭	
▭▭▭▭▭▭			15		▭▭▭▭▭▭	
▭▭▭▭▭▭			16		▭▭▭▭▭▭	
▭▭▭▭▭▭			17		▭▭▭▭▭▭	
▭▭▭▭▭▭			18		▭▭▭▭▭▭	
▭▭▭▭▭▭			19		▭▭▭▭▭▭	
▭▭▭▭▭▭			20		▭▭▭▭▭▭	
Tiles + or −					Tiles + or −	
Overtime Penalty					Overtime Penalty	
Final Score					**Final Score**	

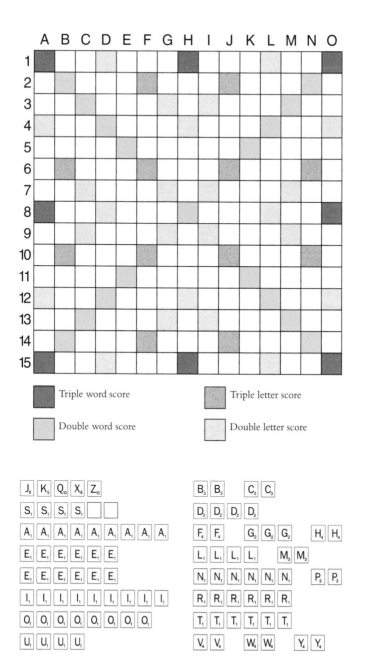

Date _____ Round 1 2 3 4 5 6 7 8 9 10 11 12 _____

Location _____

Rating	P1			P2		Rating
			1			
			2			
			3			
			4			
			5			
			6			
			7			
			8			
			9			
			10			
			11			
			12			
			13			
			14			
			15			
			16			
			17			
			18			
			19			
			20			
Tiles + or −				Tiles + or −		
Overtime Penalty				Overtime Penalty		
Final Score				**Final Score**		

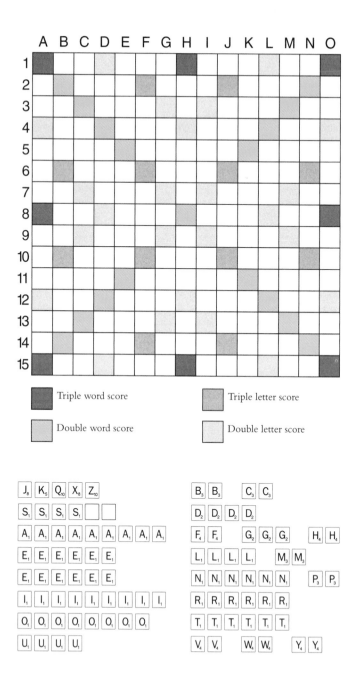

Date _____ Round 1 2 3 4 5 6 7 8 9 10 11 12 _____
Location _____

Rating	P1				P2		Rating
			1				
			2				
			3				
			4				
			5				
			6				
			7				
			8				
			9				
			10				
			11				
			12				
			13				
			14				
			15				
			16				
			17				
			18				
			19				
			20				
Tiles + or −					Tiles + or −		
Overtime Penalty					Overtime Penalty		
Final Score					**Final Score**		

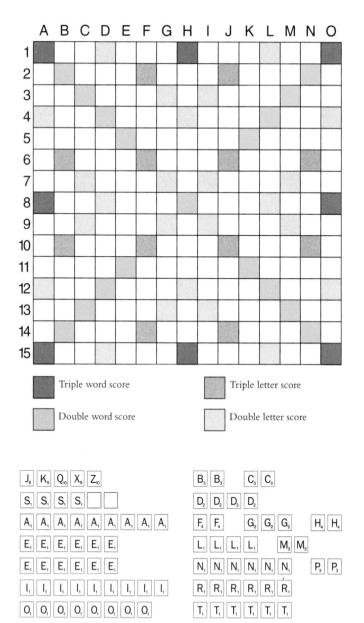

Date _____ Round 1 2 3 4 5 6 7 8 9 10 11 12 _____
Location _____

Rating	P1			P2		Rating
			1			
			2			
			3			
			4			
			5			
			6			
			7			
			8			
			9			
			10			
			11			
			12			
			13			
			14			
			15			
			16			
			17			
			18			
			19			
			20			
Tiles + or −				Tiles + or −		
Overtime Penalty				Overtime Penalty		
Final Score				**Final Score**		

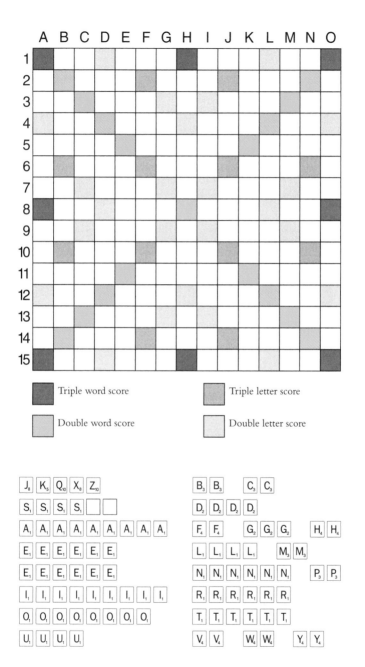

Date _____ Round 1 2 3 4 5 6 7 8 9 10 11 12 _____
Location _____

Rating	P1				P2		Rating
			1				
			2				
			3				
			4				
			5				
			6				
			7				
			8				
			9				
			10				
			11				
			12				
			13				
			14				
			15				
			16				
			17				
			18				
			19				
			20				
Tiles + or −					Tiles + or −		
Overtime Penalty					Overtime Penalty		
Final Score					**Final Score**		

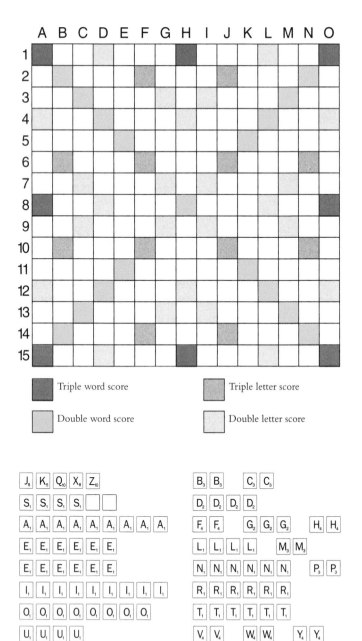

Date _____ Round 1 2 3 4 5 6 7 8 9 10 11 12 _____

Location _____

Rating	P1			P2		Rating
☐☐☐☐☐☐			**1**		☐☐☐☐☐☐	
☐☐☐☐☐☐			**2**		☐☐☐☐☐☐	
☐☐☐☐☐☐			**3**		☐☐☐☐☐☐	
☐☐☐☐☐☐			**4**		☐☐☐☐☐☐	
☐☐☐☐☐☐			**5**		☐☐☐☐☐☐	
☐☐☐☐☐☐			**6**		☐☐☐☐☐☐	
☐☐☐☐☐☐			**7**		☐☐☐☐☐☐	
☐☐☐☐☐☐			**8**		☐☐☐☐☐☐	
☐☐☐☐☐☐			**9**		☐☐☐☐☐☐	
☐☐☐☐☐☐			**10**		☐☐☐☐☐☐	
☐☐☐☐☐☐			**11**		☐☐☐☐☐☐	
☐☐☐☐☐☐			**12**		☐☐☐☐☐☐	
☐☐☐☐☐☐			**13**		☐☐☐☐☐☐	
☐☐☐☐☐☐			**14**		☐☐☐☐☐☐	
☐☐☐☐☐☐			**15**		☐☐☐☐☐☐	
☐☐☐☐☐☐			**16**		☐☐☐☐☐☐	
☐☐☐☐☐☐			**17**		☐☐☐☐☐☐	
☐☐☐☐☐☐			**18**		☐☐☐☐☐☐	
☐☐☐☐☐☐			**19**		☐☐☐☐☐☐	
☐☐☐☐☐☐			**20**		☐☐☐☐☐☐	
Tiles + or −					Tiles + or −	
Overtime Penalty					Overtime Penalty	
Final Score					**Final Score**	

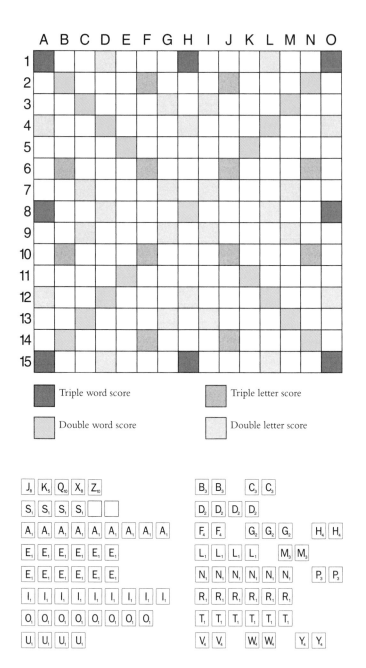

Date _____ Round 1 2 3 4 5 6 7 8 9 10 11 12 _____
Location _____

Rating	P1			P2		Rating
			1			
			2			
			3			
			4			
			5			
			6			
			7			
			8			
			9			
			10			
			11			
			12			
			13			
			14			
			15			
			16			
			17			
			18			
			19			
			20			
Tiles + or −				Tiles + or −		
Overtime Penalty				Overtime Penalty		
Final Score				**Final Score**		

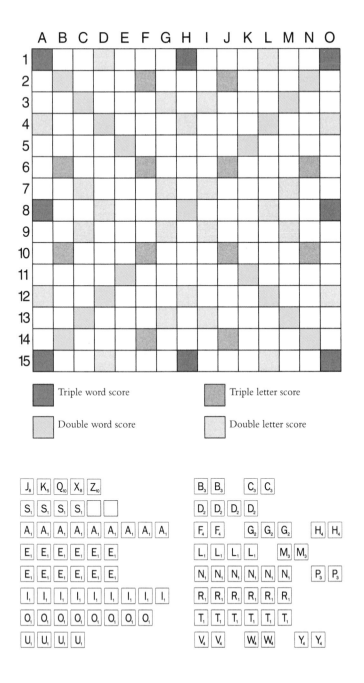

Date _____ Round 1 2 3 4 5 6 7 8 9 10 11 12 _____
Location _____

Rating	P1			P2		Rating
			1			
			2			
			3			
			4			
			5			
			6			
			7			
			8			
			9			
			10			
			11			
			12			
			13			
			14			
			15			
			16			
			17			
			18			
			19			
			20			
Tiles + or −					Tiles + or −	
Overtime Penalty					Overtime Penalty	
Final Score					**Final Score**	

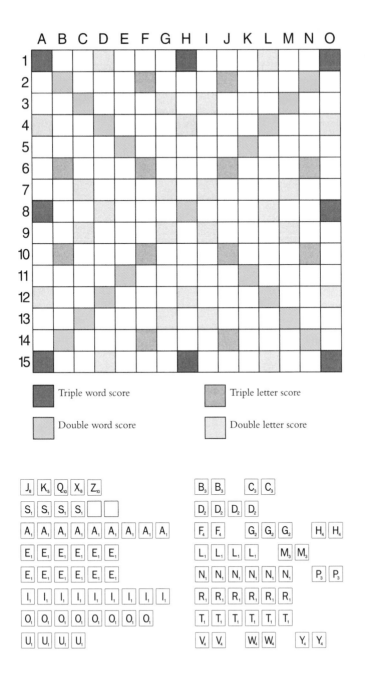

Date _____ Round 1 2 3 4 5 6 7 8 9 10 11 12 _____
Location _____

Rating	P1			P2		Rating
▭▭▭▭▭▭			**1**		▭▭▭▭▭▭	
▭▭▭▭▭▭			**2**		▭▭▭▭▭▭	
▭▭▭▭▭▭			**3**		▭▭▭▭▭▭	
▭▭▭▭▭▭			**4**		▭▭▭▭▭▭	
▭▭▭▭▭▭			**5**		▭▭▭▭▭▭	
▭▭▭▭▭▭			**6**		▭▭▭▭▭▭	
▭▭▭▭▭▭			**7**		▭▭▭▭▭▭	
▭▭▭▭▭▭			**8**		▭▭▭▭▭▭	
▭▭▭▭▭▭			**9**		▭▭▭▭▭▭	
▭▭▭▭▭▭			**10**		▭▭▭▭▭▭	
▭▭▭▭▭▭			**11**		▭▭▭▭▭▭	
▭▭▭▭▭▭			**12**		▭▭▭▭▭▭	
▭▭▭▭▭▭			**13**		▭▭▭▭▭▭	
▭▭▭▭▭▭			**14**		▭▭▭▭▭▭	
▭▭▭▭▭▭			**15**		▭▭▭▭▭▭	
▭▭▭▭▭▭			**16**		▭▭▭▭▭▭	
▭▭▭▭▭▭			**17**		▭▭▭▭▭▭	
▭▭▭▭▭▭			**18**		▭▭▭▭▭▭	
▭▭▭▭▭▭			**19**		▭▭▭▭▭▭	
▭▭▭▭▭▭			**20**		▭▭▭▭▭▭	
Tiles + or −				Tiles + or −		
Overtime Penalty				Overtime Penalty		
Final Score				**Final Score**		

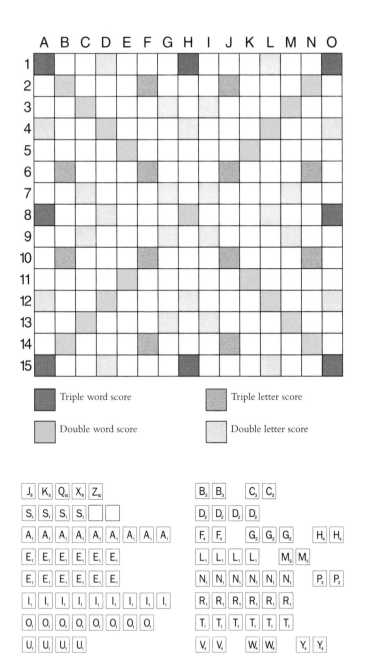

Date _____ Round 1 2 3 4 5 6 7 8 9 10 11 12 _____

Location _____

Rating	P1			P2		Rating
			1			
			2			
			3			
			4			
			5			
			6			
			7			
			8			
			9			
			10			
			11			
			12			
			13			
			14			
			15			
			16			
			17			
			18			
			19			
			20			
Tiles + or −					Tiles + or −	
Overtime Penalty					Overtime Penalty	
Final Score					**Final Score**	

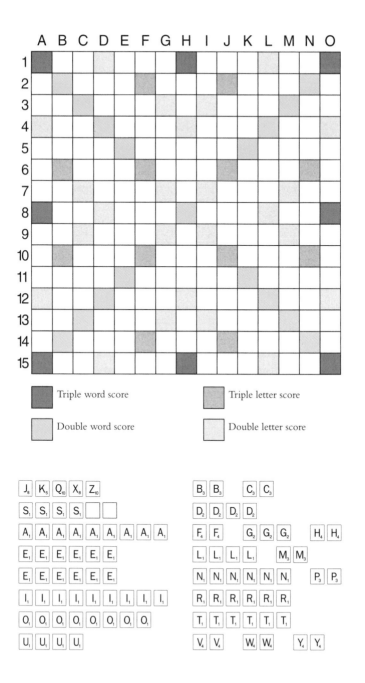

Date _____ Round 1 2 3 4 5 6 7 8 9 10 11 12 _____
Location _____

Rating	P1			P2		Rating
			1			
			2			
			3			
			4			
			5			
			6			
			7			
			8			
			9			
			10			
			11			
			12			
			13			
			14			
			15			
			16			
			17			
			18			
			19			
			20			
Tiles + or −				Tiles + or −		
Overtime Penalty				Overtime Penalty		
Final Score				**Final Score**		

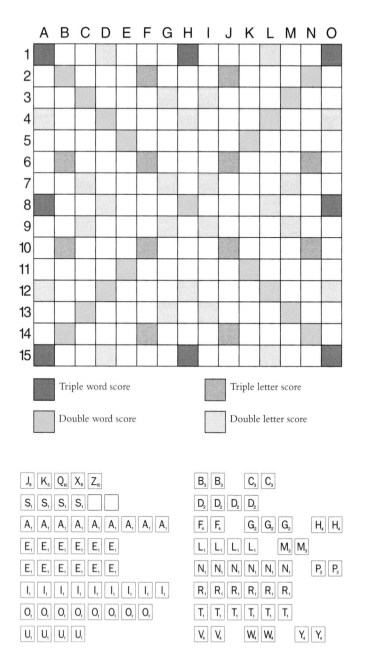

Date _____ Round 1 2 3 4 5 6 7 8 9 10 11 12 _____
Location _____

Rating	P1				P2		Rating
			1				
			2				
			3				
			4				
			5				
			6				
			7				
			8				
			9				
			10				
			11				
			12				
			13				
			14				
			15				
			16				
			17				
			18				
			19				
			20				
Tiles + or −				Tiles + or −			
Overtime Penalty				Overtime Penalty			
Final Score				**Final Score**			

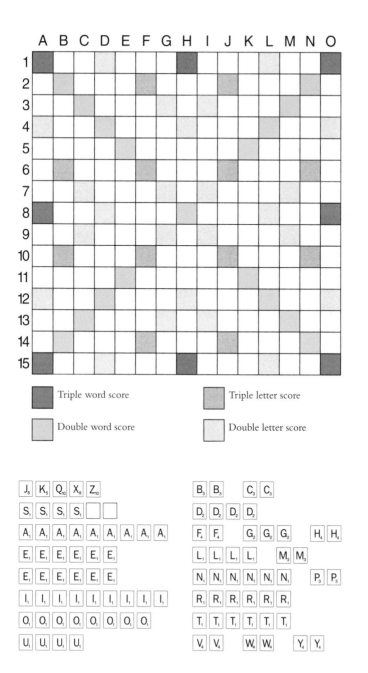

Date _____ Round 1 2 3 4 5 6 7 8 9 10 11 12 _____

Location _____

Rating	P1		P2		Rating
☐☐☐☐☐☐		1		☐☐☐☐☐☐	
☐☐☐☐☐☐		2		☐☐☐☐☐☐	
☐☐☐☐☐☐		3		☐☐☐☐☐☐	
☐☐☐☐☐☐		4		☐☐☐☐☐☐	
☐☐☐☐☐☐		5		☐☐☐☐☐☐	
☐☐☐☐☐☐		6		☐☐☐☐☐☐	
☐☐☐☐☐☐		7		☐☐☐☐☐☐	
☐☐☐☐☐☐		8		☐☐☐☐☐☐	
☐☐☐☐☐☐		9		☐☐☐☐☐☐	
☐☐☐☐☐☐		10		☐☐☐☐☐☐	
☐☐☐☐☐☐		11		☐☐☐☐☐☐	
☐☐☐☐☐☐		12		☐☐☐☐☐☐	
☐☐☐☐☐☐		13		☐☐☐☐☐☐	
☐☐☐☐☐☐		14		☐☐☐☐☐☐	
☐☐☐☐☐☐		15		☐☐☐☐☐☐	
☐☐☐☐☐☐		16		☐☐☐☐☐☐	
☐☐☐☐☐☐		17		☐☐☐☐☐☐	
☐☐☐☐☐☐		18		☐☐☐☐☐☐	
☐☐☐☐☐☐		19		☐☐☐☐☐☐	
☐☐☐☐☐☐		20		☐☐☐☐☐☐	
Tiles + or −				Tiles + or −	
Overtime Penalty				Overtime Penalty	
Final Score				**Final Score**	

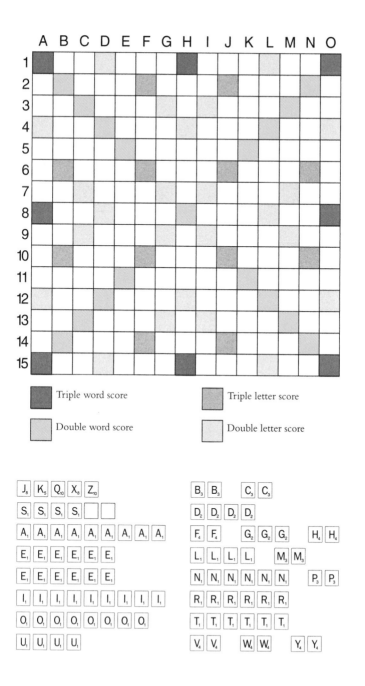

Date _____ Round 1 2 3 4 5 6 7 8 9 10 11 12 _____
Location _____

Rating	P1				P2		Rating
			1				
			2				
			3				
			4				
			5				
			6				
			7				
			8				
			9				
			10				
			11				
			12				
			13				
			14				
			15				
			16				
			17				
			18				
			19				
			20				
Tiles + or −					Tiles + or −		
Overtime Penalty					Overtime Penalty		
Final Score					**Final Score**		

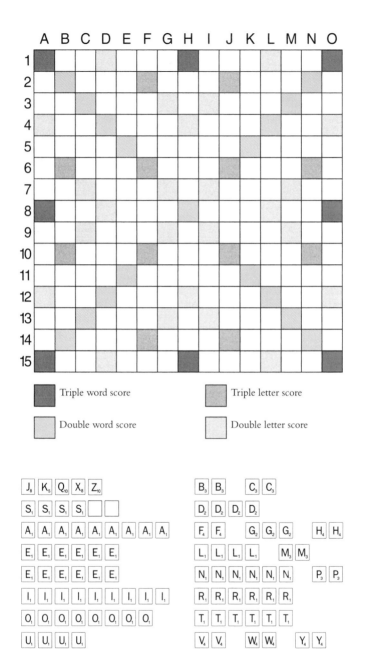

Date _____ Round 1 2 3 4 5 6 7 8 9 10 11 12 _____
Location _____

Rating	P1			P2		Rating
			1			
			2			
			3			
			4			
			5			
			6			
			7			
			8			
			9			
			10			
			11			
			12			
			13			
			14			
			15			
			16			
			17			
			18			
			19			
			20			
Tiles + or −					Tiles + or −	
Overtime Penalty					Overtime Penalty	
Final Score					**Final Score**	

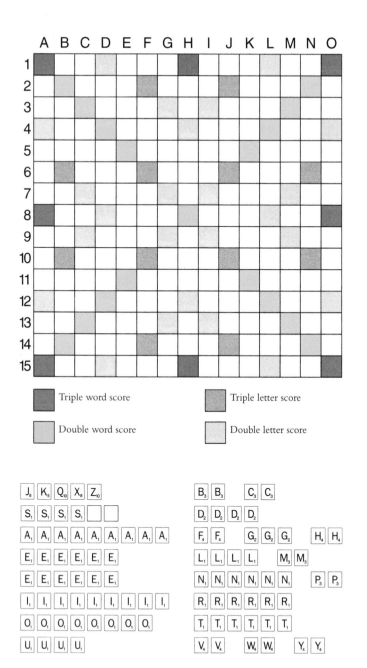

Date _____ Round 1 2 3 4 5 6 7 8 9 10 11 12 _____

Location _____

Rating	P1				P2		Rating
			1				
			2				
			3				
			4				
			5				
			6				
			7				
			8				
			9				
			10				
			11				
			12				
			13				
			14				
			15				
			16				
			17				
			18				
			19				
			20				
Tiles + or −					Tiles + or −		
Overtime Penalty					Overtime Penalty		
Final Score					**Final Score**		

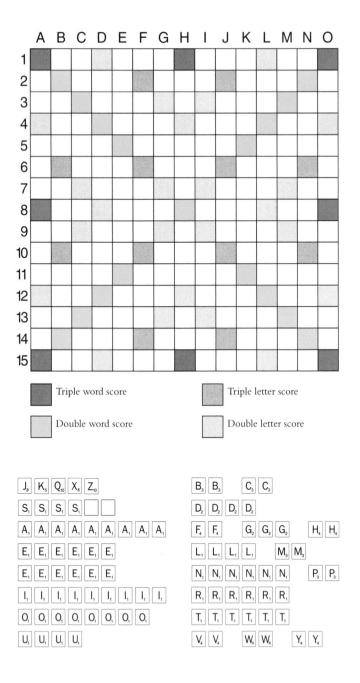

Date _____ Round 1 2 3 4 5 6 7 8 9 10 11 12 _____
Location _____

Rating	P1			P2		Rating
			1			
			2			
			3			
			4			
			5			
			6			
			7			
			8			
			9			
			10			
			11			
			12			
			13			
			14			
			15			
			16			
			17			
			18			
			19			
			20			
Tiles + or −				Tiles + or −		
Overtime Penalty				Overtime Penalty		
Final Score				**Final Score**		

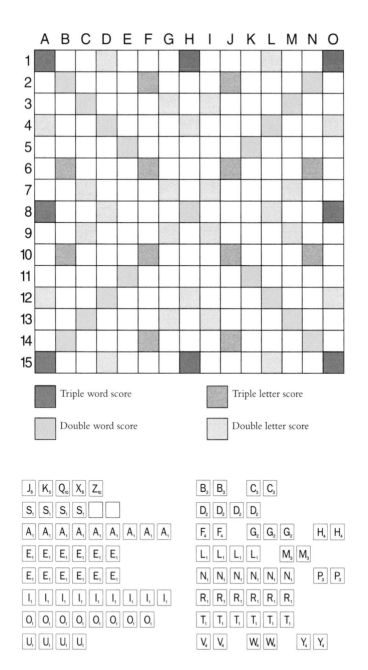

Date _____ Round 1 2 3 4 5 6 7 8 9 10 11 12 _____
Location _____

Rating	P1			P2		Rating
			1			
			2			
			3			
			4			
			5			
			6			
			7			
			8			
			9			
			10			
			11			
			12			
			13			
			14			
			15			
			16			
			17			
			18			
			19			
			20			
Tiles + or −					Tiles + or −	
Overtime Penalty					Overtime Penalty	
Final Score					**Final Score**	

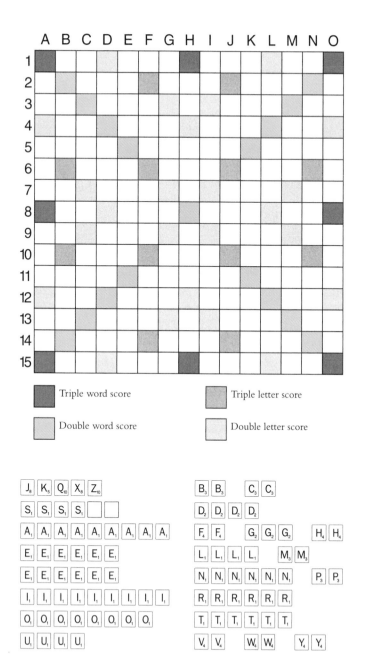

Date _____ Round 1 2 3 4 5 6 7 8 9 10 11 12 _____
Location _____

Rating	P1			P2		Rating
			1			
			2			
			3			
			4			
			5			
			6			
			7			
			8			
			9			
			10			
			11			
			12			
			13			
			14			
			15			
			16			
			17			
			18			
			19			
			20			
Tiles + or −				Tiles + or −		
Overtime Penalty				Overtime Penalty		
Final Score				**Final Score**		

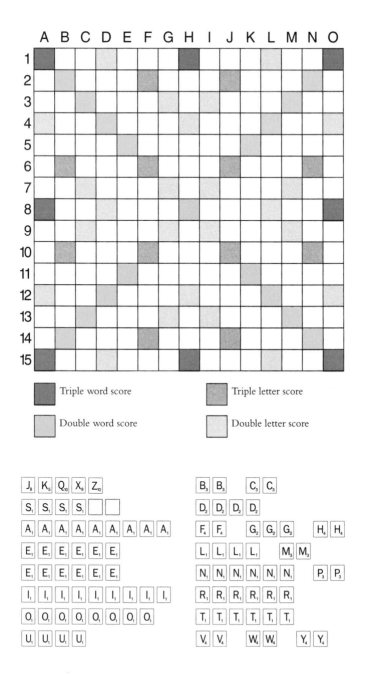

Date _____ Round 1 2 3 4 5 6 7 8 9 10 11 12 _____
Location _____

Rating	P1			P2		Rating
			1			
			2			
			3			
			4			
			5			
			6			
			7			
			8			
			9			
			10			
			11			
			12			
			13			
			14			
			15			
			16			
			17			
			18			
			19			
			20			
Tiles + or −				Tiles + or −		
Overtime Penalty				Overtime Penalty		
Final Score				**Final Score**		

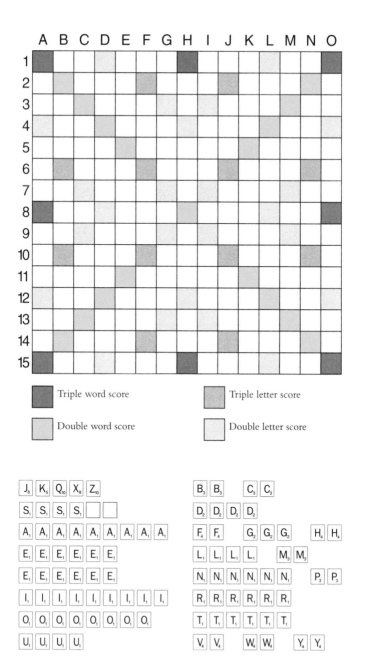

Date _____ Round 1 2 3 4 5 6 7 8 9 10 11 12 _____
Location _____

Rating	P1			P2		Rating
▭▭▭▭▭▭			**1**			▭▭▭▭▭▭
▭▭▭▭▭▭			**2**			▭▭▭▭▭▭
▭▭▭▭▭▭			**3**			▭▭▭▭▭▭
▭▭▭▭▭▭			**4**			▭▭▭▭▭▭
▭▭▭▭▭▭			**5**			▭▭▭▭▭▭
▭▭▭▭▭▭			**6**			▭▭▭▭▭▭
▭▭▭▭▭▭			**7**			▭▭▭▭▭▭
▭▭▭▭▭▭			**8**			▭▭▭▭▭▭
▭▭▭▭▭▭			**9**			▭▭▭▭▭▭
▭▭▭▭▭▭			**10**			▭▭▭▭▭▭
▭▭▭▭▭▭			**11**			▭▭▭▭▭▭
▭▭▭▭▭▭			**12**			▭▭▭▭▭▭
▭▭▭▭▭▭			**13**			▭▭▭▭▭▭
▭▭▭▭▭▭			**14**			▭▭▭▭▭▭
▭▭▭▭▭▭			**15**			▭▭▭▭▭▭
▭▭▭▭▭▭			**16**			▭▭▭▭▭▭
▭▭▭▭▭▭			**17**			▭▭▭▭▭▭
▭▭▭▭▭▭			**18**			▭▭▭▭▭▭
▭▭▭▭▭▭			**19**			▭▭▭▭▭▭
▭▭▭▭▭▭			**20**			▭▭▭▭▭▭
Tiles + or −				Tiles + or −		
Overtime Penalty				Overtime Penalty		
Final Score				**Final Score**		

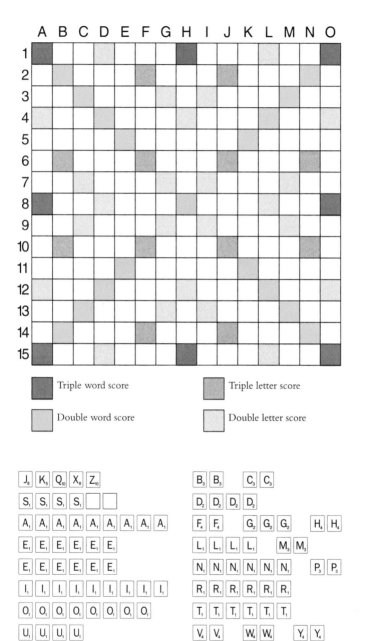

Date _____ Round 1 2 3 4 5 6 7 8 9 10 11 12 _____
Location _____

Rating	P1				P2		Rating
			1				
			2				
			3				
			4				
			5				
			6				
			7				
			8				
			9				
			10				
			11				
			12				
			13				
			14				
			15				
			16				
			17				
			18				
			19				
			20				
Tiles + or −					Tiles + or −		
Overtime Penalty					Overtime Penalty		
Final Score					**Final Score**		

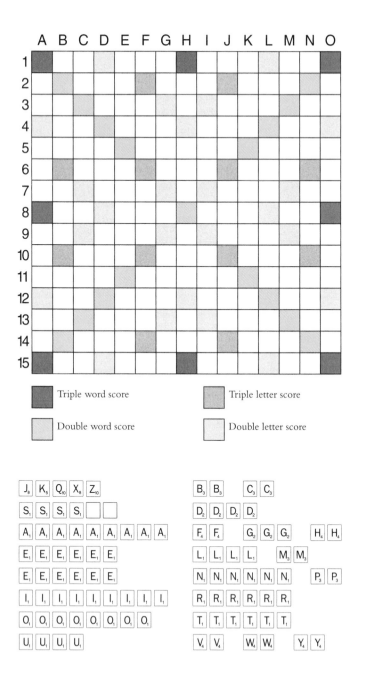

Date _____ Round 1 2 3 4 5 6 7 8 9 10 11 12 _____
Location _____

Rating	P1			P2		Rating
			1			
			2			
			3			
			4			
			5			
			6			
			7			
			8			
			9			
			10			
			11			
			12			
			13			
			14			
			15			
			16			
			17			
			18			
			19			
			20			
Tiles + or −				Tiles + or −		
Overtime Penalty				Overtime Penalty		
Final Score				**Final Score**		

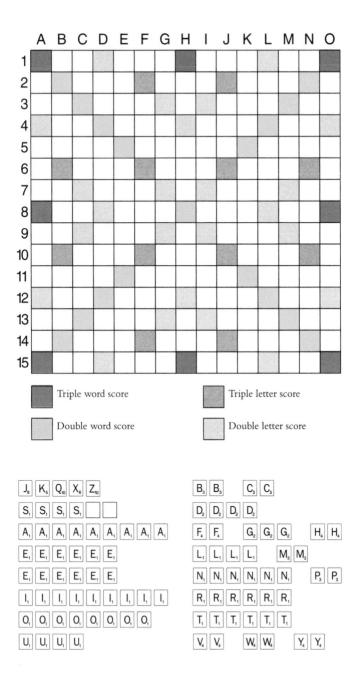

Date _____ Round 1 2 3 4 5 6 7 8 9 10 11 12 _____
Location _____

Rating	P1			P2		Rating
▢▢▢▢▢▢			**1**		▢▢▢▢▢▢	
▢▢▢▢▢▢			**2**		▢▢▢▢▢▢	
▢▢▢▢▢▢			**3**		▢▢▢▢▢▢	
▢▢▢▢▢▢			**4**		▢▢▢▢▢▢	
▢▢▢▢▢▢			**5**		▢▢▢▢▢▢	
▢▢▢▢▢▢			**6**		▢▢▢▢▢▢	
▢▢▢▢▢▢			**7**		▢▢▢▢▢▢	
▢▢▢▢▢▢			**8**		▢▢▢▢▢▢	
▢▢▢▢▢▢			**9**		▢▢▢▢▢▢	
▢▢▢▢▢▢			**10**		▢▢▢▢▢▢	
▢▢▢▢▢▢			**11**		▢▢▢▢▢▢	
▢▢▢▢▢▢			**12**		▢▢▢▢▢▢	
▢▢▢▢▢▢			**13**		▢▢▢▢▢▢	
▢▢▢▢▢▢			**14**		▢▢▢▢▢▢	
▢▢▢▢▢▢			**15**		▢▢▢▢▢▢	
▢▢▢▢▢▢			**16**		▢▢▢▢▢▢	
▢▢▢▢▢▢			**17**		▢▢▢▢▢▢	
▢▢▢▢▢▢			**18**		▢▢▢▢▢▢	
▢▢▢▢▢▢			**19**		▢▢▢▢▢▢	
▢▢▢▢▢▢			**20**		▢▢▢▢▢▢	
Tiles + or −					Tiles + or −	
Overtime Penalty					Overtime Penalty	
Final Score					**Final Score**	

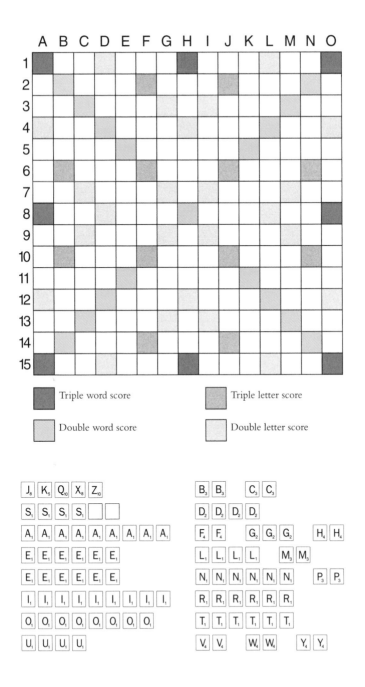

	Name	Name	Name	Name
1				
2	+	+	+	+
3	+	+	+	+
4	+	+	+	+
5	+	+	+	+
6	+	+	+	+
7	+	+	+	+
8	+	+	+	+
9	+	+	+	+
10	+	+	+	+
11	+	+	+	+
12	+	+	+	+
13	+	+	+	+
14	+	+	+	+
15	+	+	+	+
16	+	+	+	+
17	+	+	+	+
18	+	+	+	+
19	+	+	+	+
20	+	+	+	+
Tiles + or −				
Total				

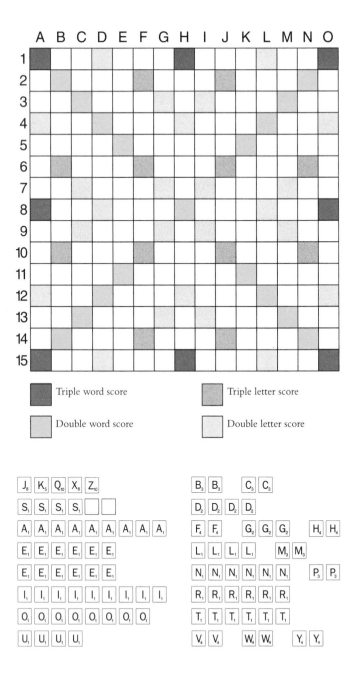

	Name	Name	Name	Name
1				
2	+	+	+	+
3	+	+	+	+
4	+	+	+	+
5	+	+	+	+
6	+	+	+	+
7	+	+	+	+
8	+	+	+	+
9	+	+	+	+
10	+	+	+	+
11	+	+	+	+
12	+	+	+	+
13	+	+	+	+
14	+	+	+	+
15	+	+	+	+
16	+	+	+	+
17	+	+	+	+
18	+	+	+	+
19	+	+	+	+
20	+	+	+	+
Tiles + or −				
Total				

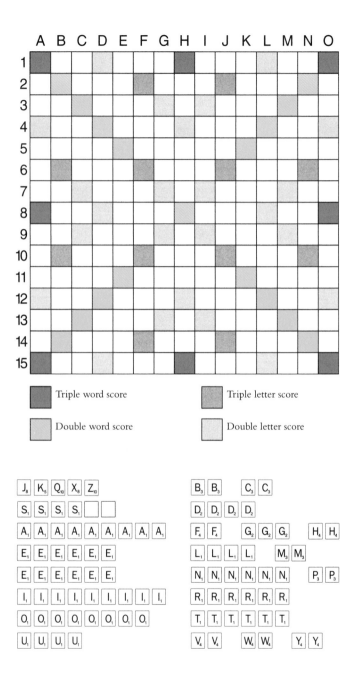

	Name	Name	Name	Name
1				
2	+	+	+	+
3	+	+	+	+
4	+	+	+	+
5	+	+	+	+
6	+	+	+	+
7	+	+	+	+
8	+	+	+	+
9	+	+	+	+
10	+	+	+	+
11	+	+	+	+
12	+	+	+	+
13	+	+	+	+
14	+	+	+	+
15	+	+	+	+
16	+	+	+	+
17	+	+	+	+
18	+	+	+	+
19	+	+	+	+
20	+	+	+	+
Tiles + or −				
Total				

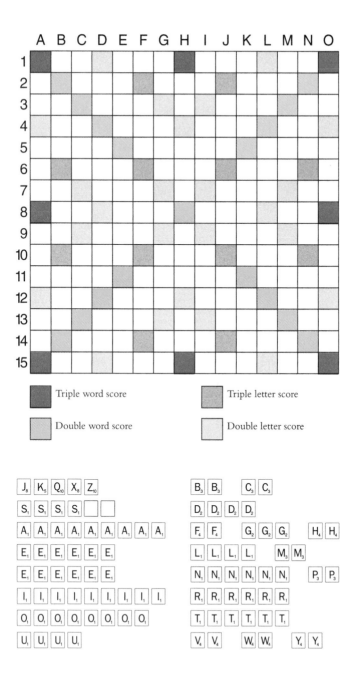

	Name	Name	Name	Name
1				
2	+	+	+	+
3	+	+	+	+
4	+	+	+	+
5	+	+	+	+
6	+	+	+	+
7	+	+	+	+
8	+	+	+	+
9	+	+	+	+
10	+	+	+	+
11	+	+	+	+
12	+	+	+	+
13	+	+	+	+
14	+	+	+	+
15	+	+	+	+
16	+	+	+	+
17	+	+	+	+
18	+	+	+	+
19	+	+	+	+
20	+	+	+	+
Tiles + or −				
Total				

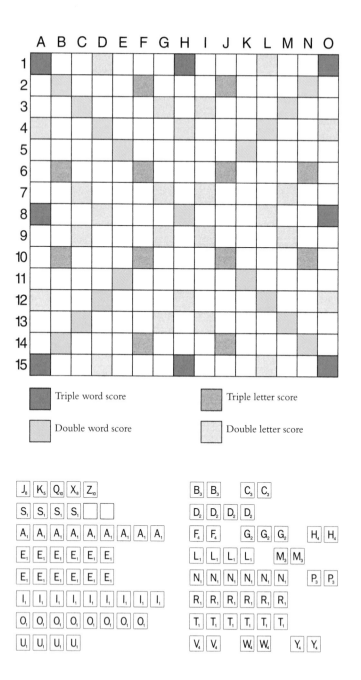

	Name	Name	Name	Name
1				
2	+	+	+	+
3	+	+	+	+
4	+	+	+	+
5	+	+	+	+
6	+	+	+	+
7	+	+	+	+
8	+	+	+	+
9	+	+	+	+
10	+	+	+	+
11	+	+	+	+
12	+	+	+	+
13	+	+	+	+
14	+	+	+	+
15	+	+	+	+
16	+	+	+	+
17	+	+	+	+
18	+	+	+	+
19	+	+	+	+
20	+	+	+	+
Tiles + or −				
Total				

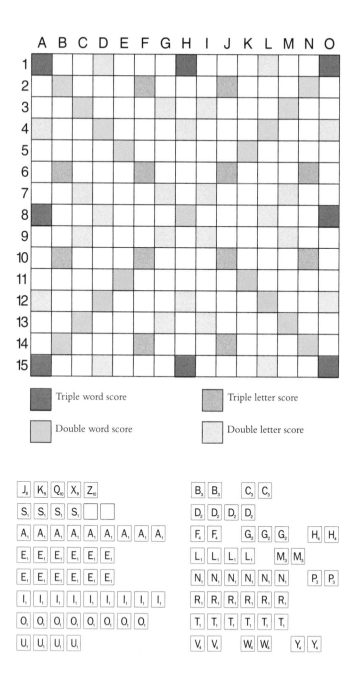

	Name	Name	Name	Name
1				
2	+	+	+	+
3	+	+	+	+
4	+	+	+	+
5	+	+	+	+
6	+	+	+	+
7	+	+	+	+
8	+	+	+	+
9	+	+	+	+
10	+	+	+	+
11	+	+	+	+
12	+	+	+	+
13	+	+	+	+
14	+	+	+	+
15	+	+	+	+
16	+	+	+	+
17	+	+	+	+
18	+	+	+	+
19	+	+	+	+
20	+	+	+	+
Tiles + or −				
Total				

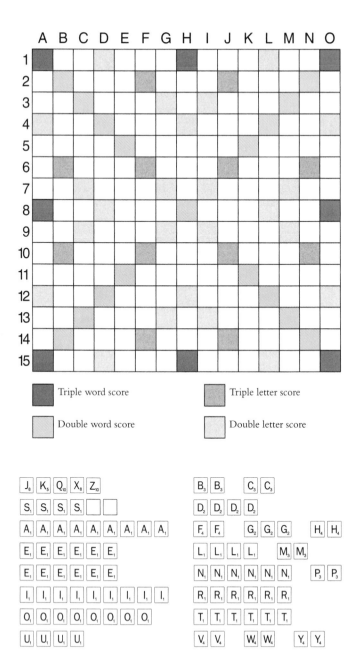

	Name	Name	Name	Name
1				
2	+	+	+	+
3	+	+	+	+
4	+	+	+	+
5	+	+	+	+
6	+	+	+	+
7	+	+	+	+
8	+	+	+	+
9	+	+	+	+
10	+	+	+	+
11	+	+	+	+
12	+	+	+	+
13	+	+	+	+
14	+	+	+	+
15	+	+	+	+
16	+	+	+	+
17	+	+	+	+
18	+	+	+	+
19	+	+	+	+
20	+	+	+	+
Tiles + or −				
Total				

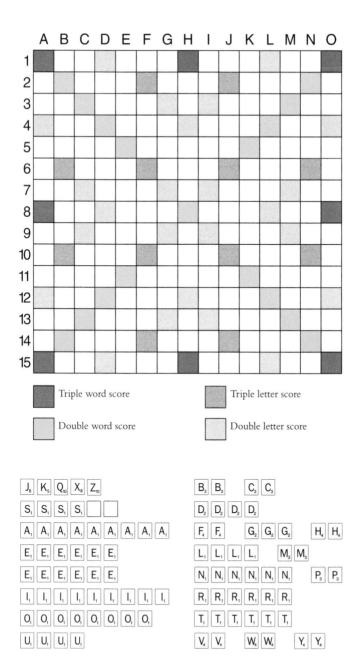

	Name	Name	Name	Name
1				
2	+	+	+	+
3	+	+	+	+
4	+	+	+	+
5	+	+	+	+
6	+	+	+	+
7	+	+	+	+
8	+	+	+	+
9	+	+	+	+
10	+	+	+	+
11	+	+	+	+
12	+	+	+	+
13	+	+	+	+
14	+	+	+	+
15	+	+	+	+
16	+	+	+	+
17	+	+	+	+
18	+	+	+	+
19	+	+	+	+
20	+	+	+	+
Tiles + or −				
Total				

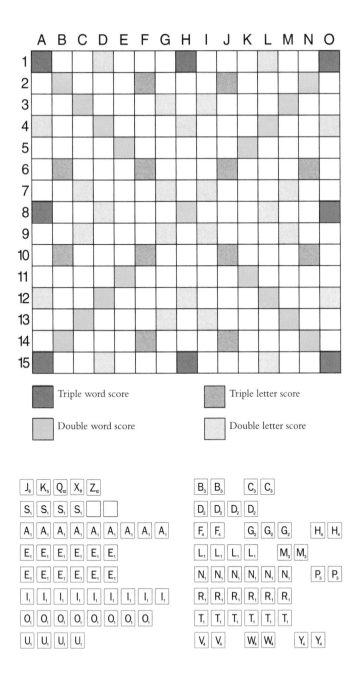

	Name	Name	Name	Name
1				
2	+	+	+	+
3	+	+	+	+
4	+	+	+	+
5	+	+	+	+
6	+	+	+	+
7	+	+	+	+
8	+	+	+	+
9	+	+	+	+
10	+	+	+	+
11	+	+	+	+
12	+	+	+	+
13	+	+	+	+
14	+	+	+	+
15	+	+	+	+
16	+	+	+	+
17	+	+	+	+
18	+	+	+	+
19	+	+	+	+
20	+	+	+	+
Tiles + or −				
Total				

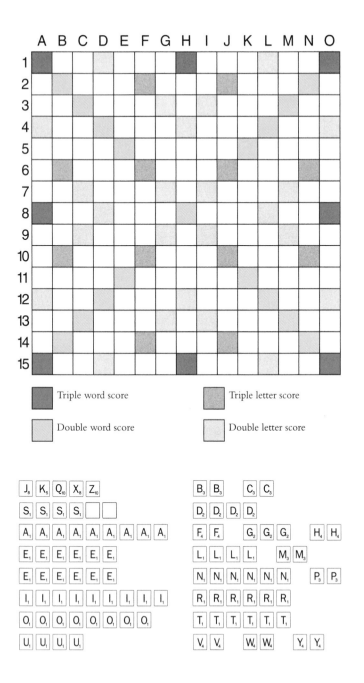

	Name	Name	Name	Name
1				
2	+	+	+	+
3	+	+	+	+
4	+	+	+	+
5	+	+	+	+
6	+	+	+	+
7	+	+	+	+
8	+	+	+	+
9	+	+	+	+
10	+	+	+	+
11	+	+	+	+
12	+	+	+	+
13	+	+	+	+
14	+	+	+	+
15	+	+	+	+
16	+	+	+	+
17	+	+	+	+
18	+	+	+	+
19	+	+	+	+
20	+	+	+	+
Tiles + or −				
Total				

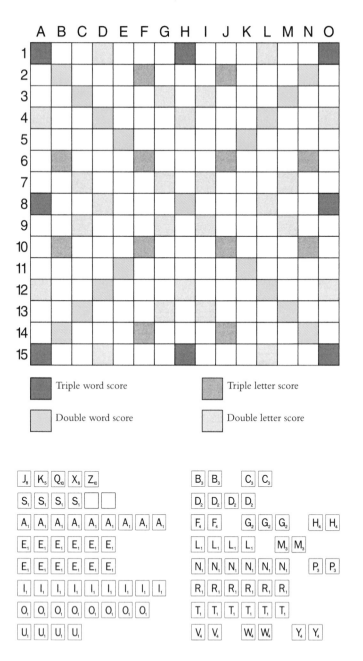

	Name	Name	Name	Name
1				
2	+	+	+	+
3	+	+	+	+
4	+	+	+	+
5	+	+	+	+
6	+	+	+	+
7	+	+	+	+
8	+	+	+	+
9	+	+	+	+
10	+	+	+	+
11	+	+	+	+
12	+	+	+	+
13	+	+	+	+
14	+	+	+	+
15	+	+	+	+
16	+	+	+	+
17	+	+	+	+
18	+	+	+	+
19	+	+	+	+
20	+	+	+	+
Tiles + or −				
Total				

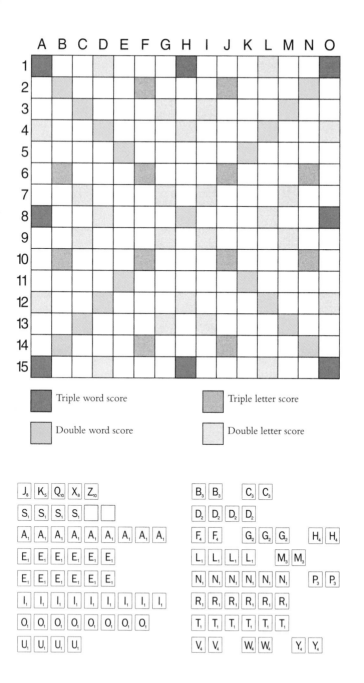

	Name	Name	Name	Name
1				
2	+	+	+	+
3	+	+	+	+
4	+	+	+	+
5	+	+	+	+
6	+	+	+	+
7	+	+	+	+
8	+	+	+	+
9	+	+	+	+
10	+	+	+	+
11	+	+	+	+
12	+	+	+	+
13	+	+	+	+
14	+	+	+	+
15	+	+	+	+
16	+	+	+	+
17	+	+	+	+
18	+	+	+	+
19	+	+	+	+
20	+	+	+	+
Tiles + or −				
Total				

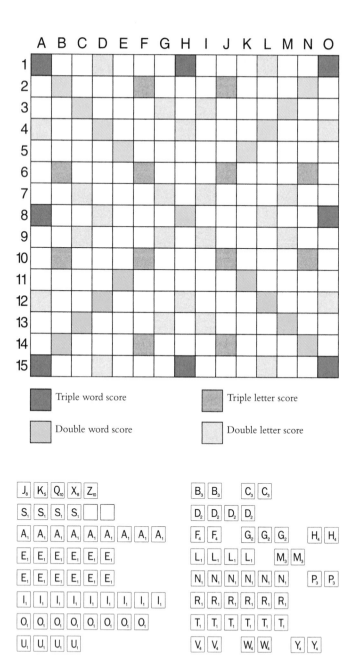

	Name	Name	Name	Name
1				
2	+	+	+	+
3	+	+	+	+
4	+	+	+	+
5	+	+	+	+
6	+	+	+	+
7	+	+	+	+
8	+	+	+	+
9	+	+	+	+
10	+	+	+	+
11	+	+	+	+
12	+	+	+	+
13	+	+	+	+
14	+	+	+	+
15	+	+	+	+
16	+	+	+	+
17	+	+	+	+
18	+	+	+	+
19	+	+	+	+
20	+	+	+	+
Tiles + or −				
Total				

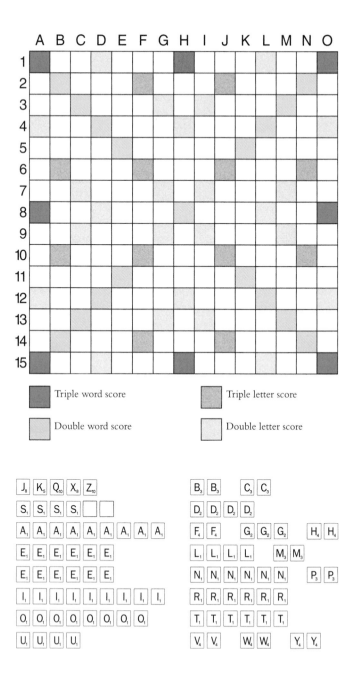

	Name	Name	Name	Name
1				
2	+	+	+	+
3	+	+	+	+
4	+	+	+	+
5	+	+	+	+
6	+	+	+	+
7	+	+	+	+
8	+	+	+	+
9	+	+	+	+
10	+	+	+	+
11	+	+	+	+
12	+	+	+	+
13	+	+	+	+
14	+	+	+	+
15	+	+	+	+
16	+	+	+	+
17	+	+	+	+
18	+	+	+	+
19	+	+	+	+
20	+	+	+	+
Tiles + or −				
Total				

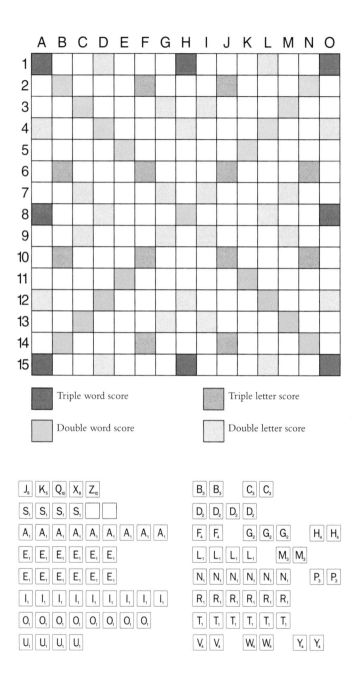

	Name	Name	Name	Name
1				
2	+	+	+	+
3	+	+	+	+
4	+	+	+	+
5	+	+	+	+
6	+	+	+	+
7	+	+	+	+
8	+	+	+	+
9	+	+	+	+
10	+	+	+	+
11	+	+	+	+
12	+	+	+	+
13	+	+	+	+
14	+	+	+	+
15	+	+	+	+
16	+	+	+	+
17	+	+	+	+
18	+	+	+	+
19	+	+	+	+
20	+	+	+	+
Tiles + or −				
Total				

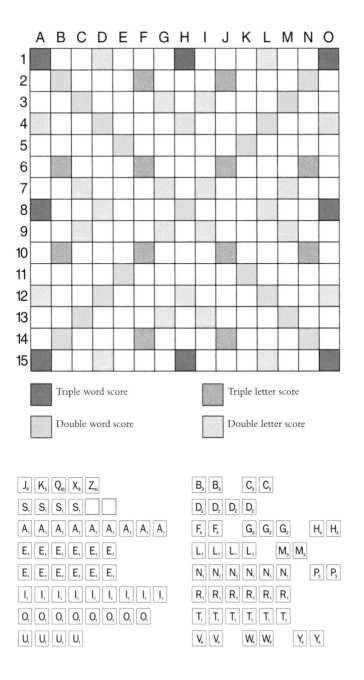

	Name	Name	Name	Name
1				
2	+	+	+	+
3	+	+	+	+
4	+	+	+	+
5	+	+	+	+
6	+	+	+	+
7	+	+	+	+
8	+	+	+	+
9	+	+	+	+
10	+	+	+	+
11	+	+	+	+
12	+	+	+	+
13	+	+	+	+
14	+	+	+	+
15	+	+	+	+
16	+	+	+	+
17	+	+	+	+
18	+	+	+	+
19	+	+	+	+
20	+	+	+	+
Tiles + or −				
Total				

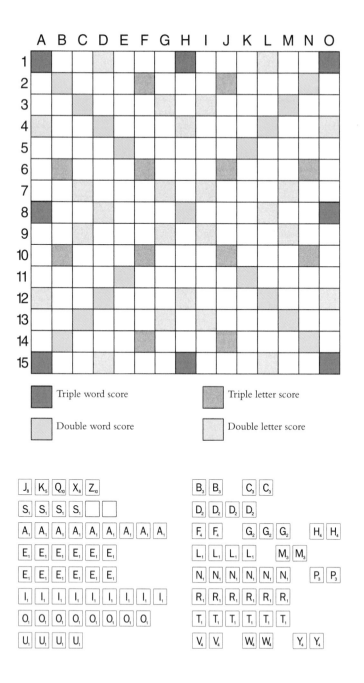

	Name	Name	Name	Name
1				
2	+	+	+	+
3	+	+	+	+
4	+	+	+	+
5	+	+	+	+
6	+	+	+	+
7	+	+	+	+
8	+	+	+	+
9	+	+	+	+
10	+	+	+	+
11	+	+	+	+
12	+	+	+	+
13	+	+	+	+
14	+	+	+	+
15	+	+	+	+
16	+	+	+	+
17	+	+	+	+
18	+	+	+	+
19	+	+	+	+
20	+	+	+	+
Tiles + or −				
Total				

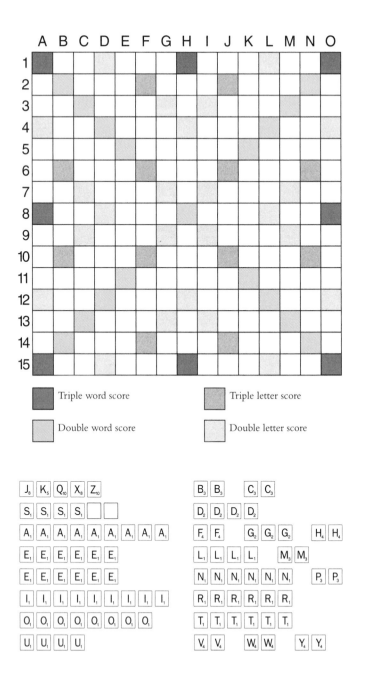

	Name	Name	Name	Name
1				
2	+	+	+	+
3	+	+	+	+
4	+	+	+	+
5	+	+	+	+
6	+	+	+	+
7	+	+	+	+
8	+	+	+	+
9	+	+	+	+
10	+	+	+	+
11	+	+	+	+
12	+	+	+	+
13	+	+	+	+
14	+	+	+	+
15	+	+	+	+
16	+	+	+	+
17	+	+	+	+
18	+	+	+	+
19	+	+	+	+
20	+	+	+	+
Tiles + or −				
Total				

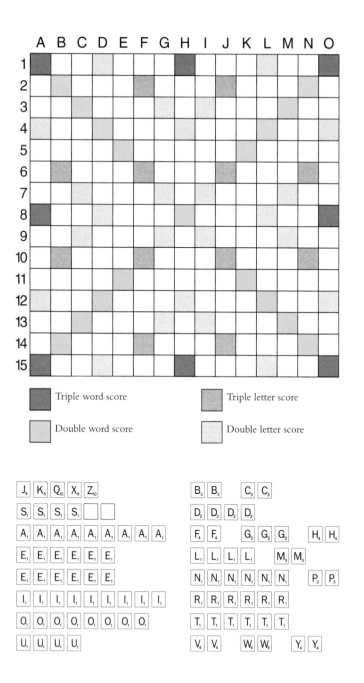

	Name	Name	Name	Name
1				
2	+	+	+	+
3	+	+	+	+
4	+	+	+	+
5	+	+	+	+
6	+	+	+	+
7	+	+	+	+
8	+	+	+	+
9	+	+	+	+
10	+	+	+	+
11	+	+	+	+
12	+	+	+	+
13	+	+	+	+
14	+	+	+	+
15	+	+	+	+
16	+	+	+	+
17	+	+	+	+
18	+	+	+	+
19	+	+	+	+
20	+	+	+	+
Tiles + or −				
Total				

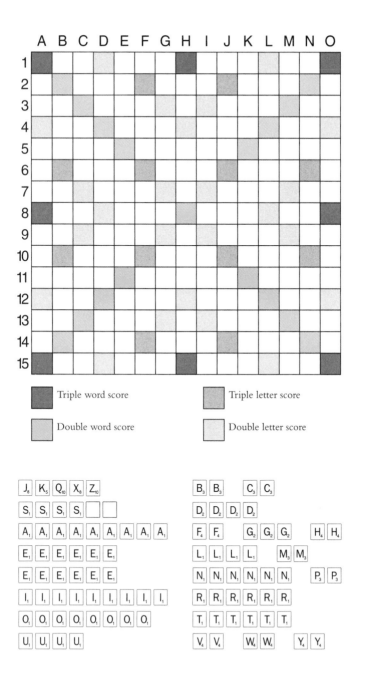

	Name	Name	Name	Name
1				
2	+	+	+	+
3	+	+	+	+
4	+	+	+	+
5	+	+	+	+
6	+	+	+	+
7	+	+	+	+
8	+	+	+	+
9	+	+	+	+
10	+	+	+	+
11	+	+	+	+
12	+	+	+	+
13	+	+	+	+
14	+	+	+	+
15	+	+	+	+
16	+	+	+	+
17	+	+	+	+
18	+	+	+	+
19	+	+	+	+
20	+	+	+	+
Tiles + or −				
Total				

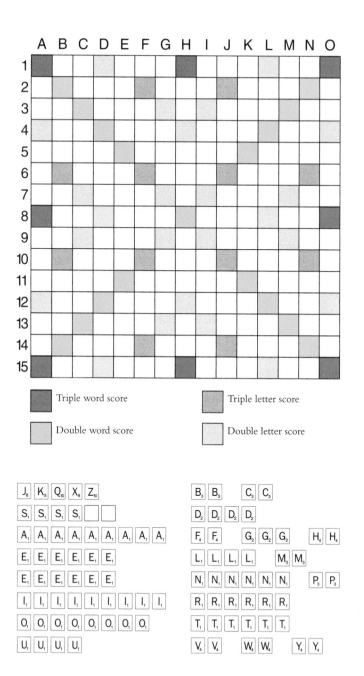

	Name	Name	Name	Name
1				
2	+	+	+	+
3	+	+	+	+
4	+	+	+	+
5	+	+	+	+
6	+	+	+	+
7	+	+	+	+
8	+	+	+	+
9	+	+	+	+
10	+	+	+	+
11	+	+	+	+
12	+	+	+	+
13	+	+	+	+
14	+	+	+	+
15	+	+	+	+
16	+	+	+	+
17	+	+	+	+
18	+	+	+	+
19	+	+	+	+
20	+	+	+	+
Tiles + or −				
Total				

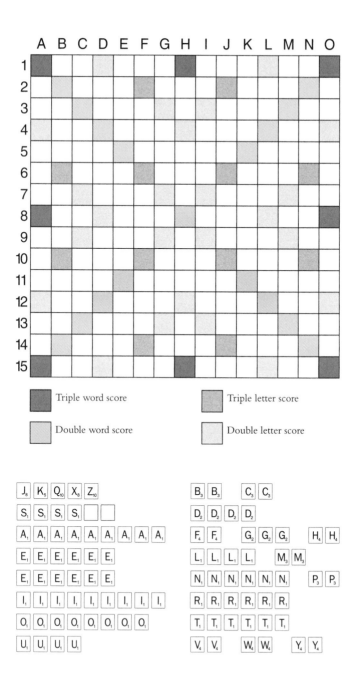

	Name	Name	Name	Name
1				
2	+	+	+	+
3	+	+	+	+
4	+	+	+	+
5	+	+	+	+
6	+	+	+	+
7	+	+	+	+
8	+	+	+	+
9	+	+	+	+
10	+	+	+	+
11	+	+	+	+
12	+	+	+	+
13	+	+	+	+
14	+	+	+	+
15	+	+	+	+
16	+	+	+	+
17	+	+	+	+
18	+	+	+	+
19	+	+	+	+
20	+	+	+	+
Tiles + or −				
Total				

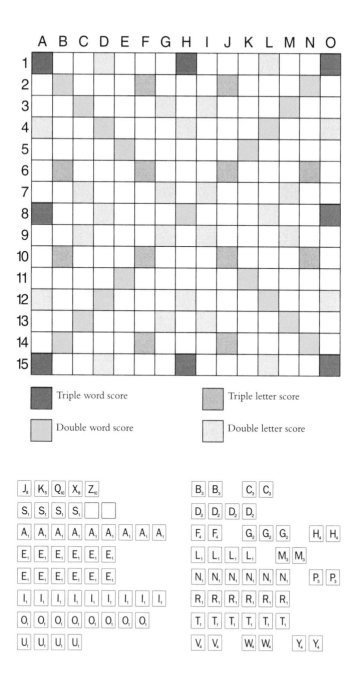

	Name	Name	Name	Name
1				
2	+	+	+	+
3	+	+	+	+
4	+	+	+	+
5	+	+	+	+
6	+	+	+	+
7	+	+	+	+
8	+	+	+	+
9	+	+	+	+
10	+	+	+	+
11	+	+	+	+
12	+	+	+	+
13	+	+	+	+
14	+	+	+	+
15	+	+	+	+
16	+	+	+	+
17	+	+	+	+
18	+	+	+	+
19	+	+	+	+
20	+	+	+	+
Tiles + or −				
Total				

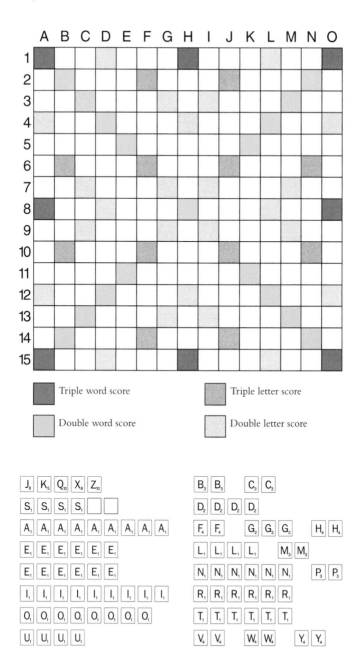

	Name	Name	Name	Name
1				
2	+	+	+	+
3	+	+	+	+
4	+	+	+	+
5	+	+	+	+
6	+	+	+	+
7	+	+	+	+
8	+	+	+	+
9	+	+	+	+
10	+	+	+	+
11	+	+	+	+
12	+	+	+	+
13	+	+	+	+
14	+	+	+	+
15	+	+	+	+
16	+	+	+	+
17	+	+	+	+
18	+	+	+	+
19	+	+	+	+
20	+	+	+	+
Tiles + or −				
Total				

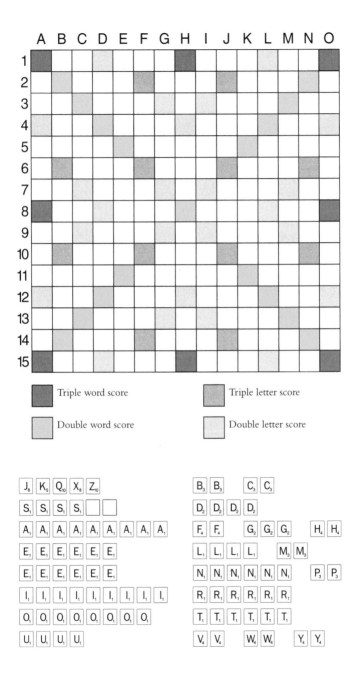

	A	B	C	D	E	F	G	H	I	J	K	L	M	N	O
1															
2															
3															
4															
5															
6															
7															
8															
9															
10															
11															
12															
13															
14															
15															

■ Triple word score   ■ Triple letter score

■ Double word score   ■ Double letter score

J_8 K_5 Q_{10} X_8 Z_{10} B_3 B_3 C_3 C_3

S_1 S_1 S_1 S_1 ☐ ☐ D_2 D_2 D_2 D_2

A_1 A_1 A_1 A_1 A_1 A_1 A_1 A_1 A_1 F_4 F_4 G_2 G_2 G_2 H_4 H_4

E_1 E_1 E_1 E_1 E_1 E_1 L_1 L_1 L_1 L_1 M_3 M_3

E_1 E_1 E_1 E_1 E_1 E_1 N_1 N_1 N_1 N_1 N_1 N_1 P_3 P_3

I_1 I_1 I_1 I_1 I_1 I_1 I_1 I_1 I_1 R_1 R_1 R_1 R_1 R_1 R_1

O_1 O_1 O_1 O_1 O_1 O_1 O_1 O_1 T_1 T_1 T_1 T_1 T_1 T_1

U_1 U_1 U_1 U_1 V_4 V_4 W_4 W_4 Y_4 Y_4

	Name	Name	Name	Name
1				
2	+	+	+	+
3	+	+	+	+
4	+	+	+	+
5	+	+	+	+
6	+	+	+	+
7	+	+	+	+
8	+	+	+	+
9	+	+	+	+
10	+	+	+	+
11	+	+	+	+
12	+	+	+	+
13	+	+	+	+
14	+	+	+	+
15	+	+	+	+
16	+	+	+	+
17	+	+	+	+
18	+	+	+	+
19	+	+	+	+
20	+	+	+	+
Tiles + or −				
Total				

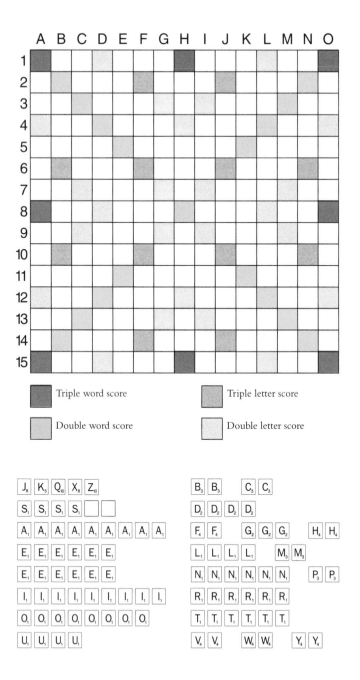

	Name	Name	Name	Name
1				
2	+	+	+	+
3	+	+	+	+
4	+	+	+	+
5	+	+	+	+
6	+	+	+	+
7	+	+	+	+
8	+	+	+	+
9	+	+	+	+
10	+	+	+	+
11	+	+	+	+
12	+	+	+	+
13	+	+	+	+
14	+	+	+	+
15	+	+	+	+
16	+	+	+	+
17	+	+	+	+
18	+	+	+	+
19	+	+	+	+
20	+	+	+	+
Tiles + or −				
Total				

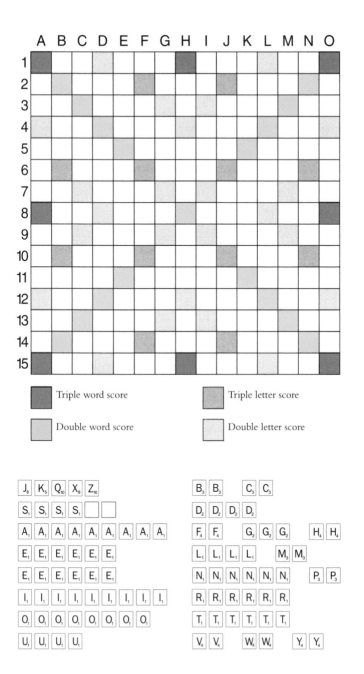

	Name	Name	Name	Name
1				
2	+	+	+	+
3	+	+	+	+
4	+	+	+	+
5	+	+	+	+
6	+	+	+	+
7	+	+	+	+
8	+	+	+	+
9	+	+	+	+
10	+	+	+	+
11	+	+	+	+
12	+	+	+	+
13	+	+	+	+
14	+	+	+	+
15	+	+	+	+
16	+	+	+	+
17	+	+	+	+
18	+	+	+	+
19	+	+	+	+
20	+	+	+	+
Tiles + or −				
Total				

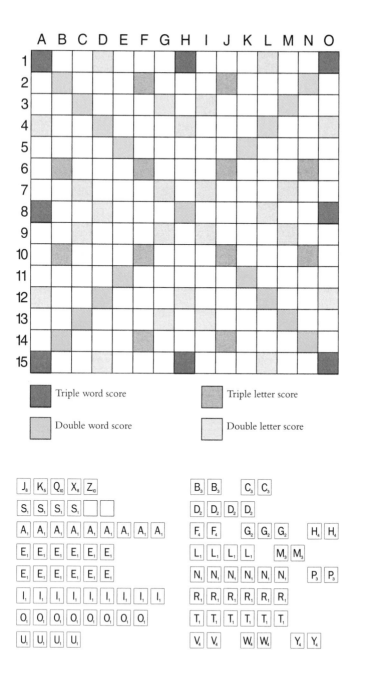

	Name	Name	Name	Name
1				
2	+	+	+	+
3	+	+	+	+
4	+	+	+	+
5	+	+	+	+
6	+	+	+	+
7	+	+	+	+
8	+	+	+	+
9	+	+	+	+
10	+	+	+	+
11	+	+	+	+
12	+	+	+	+
13	+	+	+	+
14	+	+	+	+
15	+	+	+	+
16	+	+	+	+
17	+	+	+	+
18	+	+	+	+
19	+	+	+	+
20	+	+	+	+
Tiles + or −				
Total				

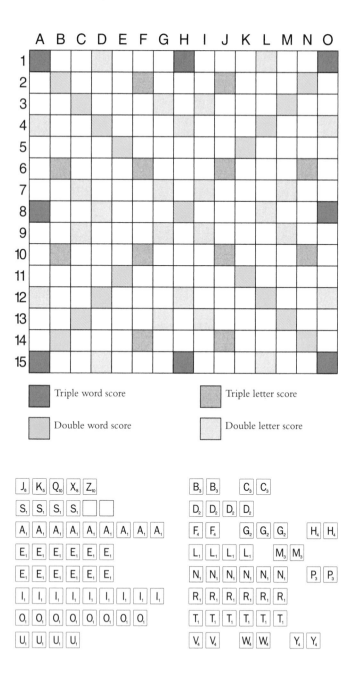

	Name	Name	Name	Name
1				
2	+	+	+	+
3	+	+	+	+
4	+	+	+	+
5	+	+	+	+
6	+	+	+	+
7	+	+	+	+
8	+	+	+	+
9	+	+	+	+
10	+	+	+	+
11	+	+	+	+
12	+	+	+	+
13	+	+	+	+
14	+	+	+	+
15	+	+	+	+
16	+	+	+	+
17	+	+	+	+
18	+	+	+	+
19	+	+	+	+
20	+	+	+	+
Tiles + or −				
Total				

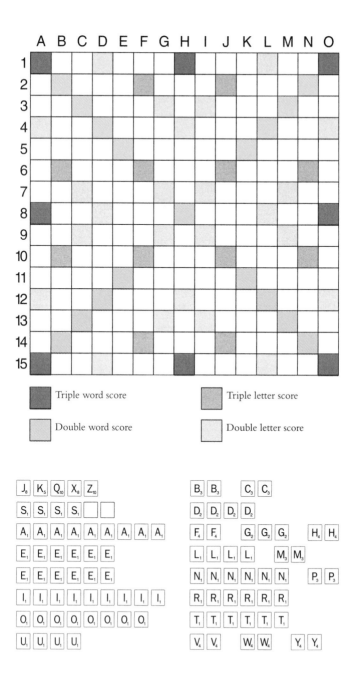

	Name	Name	Name	Name
1				
2	+	+	+	+
3	+	+	+	+
4	+	+	+	+
5	+	+	+	+
6	+	+	+	+
7	+	+	+	+
8	+	+	+	+
9	+	+	+	+
10	+	+	+	+
11	+	+	+	+
12	+	+	+	+
13	+	+	+	+
14	+	+	+	+
15	+	+	+	+
16	+	+	+	+
17	+	+	+	+
18	+	+	+	+
19	+	+	+	+
20	+	+	+	+
Tiles + or −				
Total				

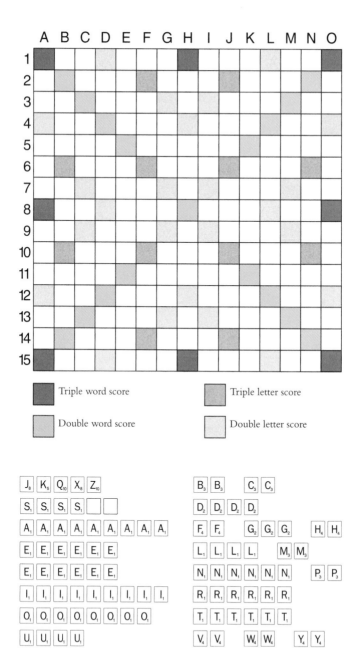

	Name	Name	Name	Name
1				
2	+	+	+	+
3	+	+	+	+
4	+	+	+	+
5	+	+	+	+
6	+	+	+	+
7	+	+	+	+
8	+	+	+	+
9	+	+	+	+
10	+	+	+	+
11	+	+	+	+
12	+	+	+	+
13	+	+	+	+
14	+	+	+	+
15	+	+	+	+
16	+	+	+	+
17	+	+	+	+
18	+	+	+	+
19	+	+	+	+
20	+	+	+	+
Tiles + or −				
Total				

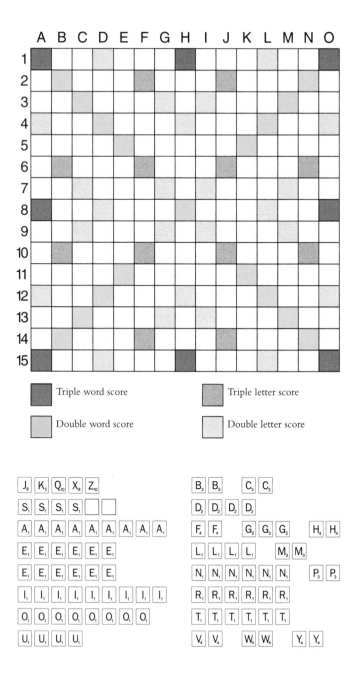

	Name	Name	Name	Name
1				
2	+	+	+	+
3	+	+	+	+
4	+	+	+	+
5	+	+	+	+
6	+	+	+	+
7	+	+	+	+
8	+	+	+	+
9	+	+	+	+
10	+	+	+	+
11	+	+	+	+
12	+	+	+	+
13	+	+	+	+
14	+	+	+	+
15	+	+	+	+
16	+	+	+	+
17	+	+	+	+
18	+	+	+	+
19	+	+	+	+
20	+	+	+	+
Tiles + or −				
Total				

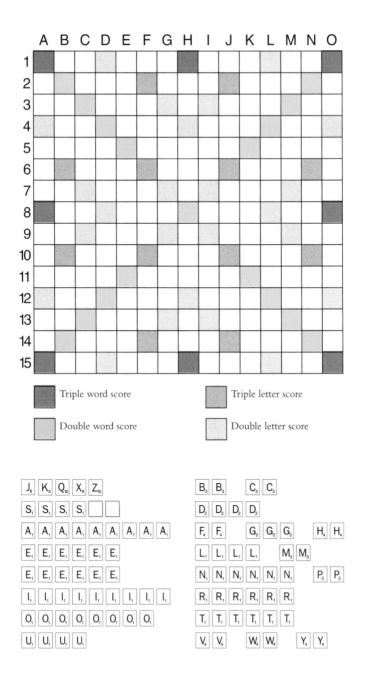

TWO-LETTER WORDS AND THEIR HOOKS

Here are all two-letter words, from AA to ZA. Next to each word are the letters that "hook" onto the word to make a three-letter word. For example, adding B to the front of AA makes BAA, and adding H, L, or S to the back of AA makes AAH, AAL, or AAS.

Front	Word	Back
B	AA	HLS
CDFGJKLNSTW	AB	ASY
BCDFGHLMPRSTW	AD	DOSZ
GHKMNSTW	AE	
BDFGHJLMNRSTWYZ	AG	AEOS
ABDHNPRY	AH	AIS
R	AI	DLMNRST
ABDGPS	AL	ABELPST
BCDGHJLNPRTY	AM	AIPU
BCDFGMNPRTVW	AN	ADEITY
BCEFGJLMOPTVWY	AR	BCEFKMST
ABFGHKLMPRTVWZ	AS	HKPS
BCEFGHKLMOPQRSTVW	AT	ET
CDHJLMNPRSTVWY	AW	AELN
FLMPRSTWZ	AX	E
BCDFGHJKLMNPRSWY	AY	ES
	AO	BA	ADGHLMNPRSTY
	BE	DEGLNSTY
	BI	BDGNOSTZ
	BO	ABDGOPSTWXY
A	BY	ES
O	DE	BEFLNVWXY
AU	DO	CEGLMNRSTW
BFGLMPRTWZ	ED	HS
DKR	EF	FST
FHPY	EH	
BCDEGMST	EL	DFKLMS
FGHMR	EM	ESU
BDFGHKMPSTWY	EN	DGS
FHPS	ER	AEGNRS
BFHOPRY	ES	S
BFGHJLMNPRSTVWY	ET	AH
DHKLRSV	EX	
	FA	BDGNRSTXY
	FE	DEHMNRSTUWYZ
AE	GO	ABDORSTX
ASW	HA	DEGHJMOPSTWY
ST	HE	HMNPRSTWXY
ACGKP	HI	DEMNPST
O	HM	M
MORTW	HO	BDEGNPTWY
ABDFGHKLMRV	ID	S
DKR	IF	FS
ABDFGHJKLPRSTWYZ	IN	KNS
ABCDHKLMPQSTVWX	IS	M
ABDFGHKLNPSTWZ	IT	S
	JO	BEGTWY
OS	KA	BEFSTY
S	KI	DFNPRST
A	LA	BCDGMPRSTVWXY
	LI	BDENPST
	LO	BGOPTWX
A	MA	CDEGNPRSTWXY

Front	Word	Back
E	ME	DGLMNTW
A	MI	BCDGLMRSX
HU	MM	
	MO	ABCDGLMNOPRSTW
AE	MU	DGMNST
	MY	C
A	NA	BEGHMNPWY
AO	NE	BEGTW
O	NO	BDGHMORSTW
G	NU	BNST
BCGHMNPRSTY	OD	ADES
DFHJRTVW	OE	S
	OF	FT
FNOP	OH	MOS
KP	OI	L
DMNRSTY	OM	S
CDEFHIMSTWY	ON	EOS
BCFHKLMPST	OP	EST
CDFGKMNT	OR	ABCEST
BCDGKMNSW	OS	E
BCDHJLMNPRSTVWY	OW	ELN
BCFGLPSV	OX	OY
BCFHJST	OY	
S	PA	CDHLMNPRSTWXY
AO	PE	ACDEGHNPRSTW
	PI	ACEGNPSTUX
	QI	S
AEIO	RE	BCDEFGIMPSTVX
A	SH	AEHY
P	SI	BCMNPRSTX
	SO	BDLMNPSTUWXY
EU	TA	BDEGJMNOPRSTUVWX
	TI	CELNPST
	TO	DEGMNOPRTWY
DH	UH	
	UM	MP
BDFGHJMNPRST	UN	S
CDHPSTY	UP	OS
BJMNP	US	E
BCGHJMNOPRT	UT	AES
AEO	WE	BDENT
T	WO	EKNOSTW
	XI	S
	XU	
PR	YA	GHKMPRWY
ABDEKLPRTW	YE	AHNPSTW
	YO	BDKMNUW
	ZA	GPSX

THREE-LETTER WORDS

AAH	ABY	ADS	AGE	AHS	AIR	ALE	AMA
AAL	ACE	ADZ	AGO	AID	AIS	ALL	AMI
AAS	ACT	AFF	AGS	AIL	AIT	ALP	AMP
ABA	ADD	AFT	AHA	AIM	ALA	ALS	AMU
ABS	ADO	AGA	AHI	AIN	ALB	ALT	ANA

AND	BRA	DID	FAR	GOA	ILL	LAY	MUD
ANE	BRO	DIE	FAS	GOB	IMP	LEA	MUG
ANI	BRR	DIF	FAT	GOD	INK	LED	MUM
ANT	BUB	DIG	FAX	GOO	INN	LEE	MUN
ANY	BUD	DIM	FAY	GOR	INS	LEG	MUS
APE	BUG	DIN	FED	GOS	ION	LEI	MUT
APO	BUM	DIP	FEE	GOT	IRE	LEK	MYC
APP	BUN	DIS	FEH	GOX	IRK	LET	NAB
APT	BUR	DIT	FEM	GUL	ISM	LEU	NAE
ARB	BUS	DOC	FEN	GUM	ITS	LEV	NAG
ARC	BUT	DOE	FER	GUN	IVY	LEX	NAH
ARE	BUY	DOG	FES	GUT	JAB	LEY	NAM
ARF	BYE	DOL	FET	GUV	JAG	LIB	NAN
ARK	BYS	DOM	FEU	GUY	JAM	LID	NAP
ARM	CAB	DON	FEW	GYM	JAR	LIE	NAW
ARS	CAD	DOR	FEY	GYP	JAW	LIN	NAY
ART	CAM	DOS	FEZ	HAD	JAY	LIP	NEB
ASH	CAN	DOT	FIB	HAE	JEE	LIS	NEE
ASK	CAP	DOW	FID	HAG	JET	LIT	NEG
ASP	CAR	DRY	FIE	HAH	JEU	LOB	NET
ASS	CAT	DUB	FIG	HAJ	JIB	LOG	NEW
ATE	CAW	DUD	FIL	HAM	JIG	LOO	NIB
ATT	CAY	DUE	FIN	HAO	JIN	LOP	NIL
AUK	CEE	DUG	FIR	HAP	JOB	LOT	NIM
AVA	CEL	DUH	FIT	HAS	JOE	LOW	NIP
AVE	CEP	DUI	FIX	HAT	JOG	LOX	NIT
AVO	CHI	DUN	FIZ	HAW	JOT	LUG	NIX
AWA	CIG	DUO	FLU	HAY	JOW	LUM	NOB
AWE	CIS	DUP	FLY	HEH	JOY	LUV	NOD
AWL	COB	DYE	FOB	HEM	JUG	LUX	NOG
AWN	COD	EAR	FOE	HEN	JUN	LYE	NOH
AXE	COG	EAT	FOG	HEP	JUS	MAC	NOM
AYE	COL	EAU	FOH	HER	JUT	MAD	NOO
AYS	CON	EBB	FON	HES	KAB	MAE	NOR
AZO	COO	ECU	FOP	HET	KAE	MAG	NOS
BAA	COP	EDH	FOR	HEW	KAF	MAN	NOT
BAD	COR	EDS	FOU	HEX	KAS	MAP	NOW
BAG	COS	EEK	FOX	HEY	KAT	MAR	NTH
BAH	COT	EEL	FOY	HIC	KAY	MAS	NUB
BAL	COW	EFF	FRO	HID	KEA	MAT	NUN
BAM	COX	EFS	FRY	HIE	KEF	MAW	NUS
BAN	COY	EFT	FUB	HIM	KEG	MAX	NUT
BAP	COZ	EGG	FUD	HIN	KEN	MAY	OAF
BAR	CRU	EGO	FUG	HIP	KEP	MED	OAK
BAS	CRY	EKE	FUN	HIS	KEX	MEG	OAR
BAT	CUB	ELD	FUR	HIT	KEY	MEL	OAT
BAY	CUD	ELF	GAB	HMM	KHI	MEM	OBA
BED	CUE	ELK	GAD	HOB	KID	MEN	OBE
BEE	CUM	ELL	GAE	HOD	KIF	MET	OBI
BEG	CUP	ELM	GAG	HOE	KIN	MEW	OCA
BEL	CUR	ELS	GAL	HOG	KIP	MHO	ODA
BEN	CUT	EME	GAM	HON	KIR	MIB	ODD
BES	CWM	EMS	GAN	HOP	KIS	MIC	ODE
BET	DAB	EMU	GAP	HOT	KIT	MID	ODS
BEY	DAD	END	GAR	HOW	KOA	MIG	OES
BIB	DAG	ENG	GAS	HOY	KOB	MIL	OFF
BID	DAH	ENS	GAT	HUB	KOI	MIM	OFT
BIG	DAK	EON	GAY	HUE	KOP	MIR	OHM
BIN	DAL	ERA	GED	HUG	KOR	MIS	OHO
BIO	DAM	ERE	GEE	HUH	KOS	MIX	OHS
BIS	DAN	ERG	GEL	HUM	KUE	MOA	OIL
BIT	DAP	ERN	GEM	HUN	KYE	MOB	OKA
BIZ	DAW	ERR	GEN	HUP	LAB	MOC	OKE
BOA	DAY	ERS	GET	HUT	LAC	MOD	OLD
BOB	DEB	ESS	GEY	HYP	LAD	MOG	OLE
BOD	DEE	ETA	GHI	ICE	LAG	MOL	OMS
BOG	DEF	ETH	GIB	ICH	LAM	MOM	ONE
BOO	DEL	EVE	GID	ICK	LAP	MON	ONO
BOP	DEN	EWE	GIE	ICY	LAR	MOO	ONS
BOS	DEV	EYE	GIG	IDS	LAS	MOP	OOH
BOT	DEW	FAB	GIN	IFF	LAT	MOR	OOT
BOW	DEX	FAD	GIP	IFS	LAV	MOS	OPE
BOX	DEY	FAG	GIT	IGG	LAW	MOT	OPS
BOY	DIB	FAN	GNU	ILK	LAX	MOW	OPT

ORA	PIN	REB	SAX	SUE	TOP	VID	YAG
ORB	PIP	REC	SAY	SUK	TOR	VIE	YAH
ORC	PIS	RED	SEA	SUM	TOT	VIG	YAK
ORE	PIT	REE	SEC	SUN	TOW	VIM	YAM
ORS	PIU	REF	SEE	SUP	TOY	VIS	YAP
ORT	PIX	REG	SEG	SUQ	TRY	VOE	YAR
OSE	PLY	REI	SEI	SYN	TSK	VOW	YAW
OUD	POD	REM	SEL	TAB	TUB	VOX	YAY
OUR	POH	REP	SEN	TAD	TUG	VUG	YEA
OUT	POI	RES	SER	TAE	TUI	VUM	YEH
OVA	POL	RET	SET	TAG	TUN	WAB	YEN
OWE	POP	REV	SEW	TAJ	TUP	WAD	YEP
OWL	POT	REX	SEX	TAM	TUT	WAE	YES
OWN	POW	RHO	SHA	TAN	TUX	WAG	YET
OXO	POX	RIA	SHE	TAO	TWA	WAN	YEW
OXY	PRO	RIB	SHH	TAP	TWO	WAP	YIN
PAC	PRY	RID	SHY	TAR	TYE	WAR	YIP
PAD	PSI	RIF	SIB	TAS	UDO	WAS	YOB
PAH	PST	RIG	SIC	TAT	UGH	WAT	YOD
PAL	PUB	RIM	SIM	TAU	UKE	WAW	YOK
PAM	PUD	RIN	SIN	TAV	ULU	WAX	YOM
PAN	PUG	RIP	SIP	TAW	UMM	WAY	YON
PAP	PUL	ROB	SIR	TAX	UMP	WEB	YOU
PAR	PUN	ROC	SIS	TEA	UNS	WED	YOW
PAS	PUP	ROD	SIT	TED	UPO	WEE	YUK
PAT	PUR	ROE	SIX	TEE	UPS	WEN	YUM
PAW	PUS	ROM	SKA	TEG	URB	WET	YUP
PAX	PUT	ROT	SKI	TEL	URD	WHA	ZAG
PAY	PYA	ROW	SKY	TEN	URN	WHO	ZAP
PEA	PYE	RUB	SLY	TET	URP	WHY	ZAS
PEC	PYX	RUE	SOB	TEW	USE	WIG	ZAX
PED	QAT	RUG	SOD	THE	UTA	WIN	ZED
PEE	QIS	RUM	SOL	THO	UTE	WIS	ZEE
PEG	QUA	RUN	SOM	THY	UTS	WIT	ZEK
PEH	RAD	RUT	SON	TIC	VAC	WIZ	ZEP
PEN	RAG	RYA	SOP	TIE	VAN	WOE	ZIG
PEP	RAH	RYE	SOS	TIL	VAR	WOK	ZIN
PER	RAI	SAB	SOT	TIN	VAS	WON	ZIP
PES	RAJ	SAC	SOU	TIP	VAT	WOO	ZIT
PET	RAM	SAD	SOW	TIS	VAU	WOS	ZOA
PEW	RAN	SAE	SOX	TIT	VAV	WOT	ZOO
PHI	RAP	SAG	SOY	TOD	VAW	WOW	ZUZ
PHT	RAS	SAL	SPA	TOE	VEE	WRY	ZZZ
PIA	RAT	SAP	SPY	TOG	VEG	WUD	
PIC	RAW	SAT	SRI	TOM	VET	WYE	
PIE	RAX	SAU	STY	TON	VEX	WYN	
PIG	RAY	SAW	SUB	TOO	VIA	XIS	

TWO-, THREE-, AND FOUR-LETTER WORDS WITH J, Q, X, AND Z

J	JOY	JAIL	JEEZ	JINK	JOTS	JUTE	QUAG
JO	JUG	JAKE	JEFE	JINN	JOUK	JUTS	QUAI
HAJ	JUN	JAMB	JEHU	JINS	JOWL	KOJI	QUAY
JAB	JUS	JAMS	JELL	JINX	JOWS	MOJO	QUEY
JAG	JUT	JANE	JEON	JIVE	JOYS	PUJA	QUID
JAM	RAJ	JAPE	JERK	JIVY	JUBA	RAJA	QUIN
JAR	TAJ	JARL	JESS	JOBS	JUBE	SOJA	QUIP
JAW	AJAR	JARS	JEST	JOCK	JUCO		QUIT
JAY	AJEE	JATO	JETE	JOES	JUDO	Q	QUIZ
JEE	DJIN	JAUK	JETS	JOEY	JUGA	QI	QUOD
JET	DOJO	JAUP	JEUX	JOGS	JUGS	QAT	SUQS
JEU	FUJI	JAVA	JIAO	JOHN	JUJU	QIS	
JIB	HADJ	JAWS	JIBB	JOIN	JUKE	QUA	X
JIG	HAJI	JAYS	JIBE	JOKE	JUKU	SUQ	AX
JIN	HAJJ	JAZZ	JIBS	JOKY	JUMP	AQUA	EX
JOB	JABS	JEAN	JIFF	JOLE	JUNK	QADI	OX
JOE	JACK	JEED	JIGS	JOLT	JUPE	QAID	XI
JOG	JADE	JEEP	JILL	JOSH	JURA	QATS	XU
JOT	JAGG	JEER	JILT	JOSS	JURY	QOPH	AXE
JOW	JAGS	JEES	JIMP	JOTA	JUST	QUAD	BOX

COX	TAX	EXEC	NIXY	FEZ	CZAR	OOZE	ZEPS
DEX	TUX	EXED	ONYX	FIZ	DAZE	OOZY	ZERK
FAX	VEX	EXES	ORYX	WIZ	DITZ	ORZO	ZERO
FIX	VOX	EXIT	OXEN	ZAG	DOZE	OUZO	ZEST
FOX	WAX	EXON	OXES	ZAP	DOZY	OYEZ	ZETA
GOX	XIS	EXPO	OXID	ZAS	FAZE	PHIZ	ZIGS
HEX	ZAX	FALX	OXIM	ZAX	FIZZ	PREZ	ZILL
KEX	APEX	FAUX	PIXY	ZED	FOZY	PUTZ	ZINC
LAX	AXAL	FIXT	PLEX	ZEE	FRIZ	QUIZ	ZINE
LEX	AXED	FLAX	POXY	ZEK	FUTZ	RAZE	ZING
LOX	AXEL	FLEX	PREX	ZEP	FUZE	RAZZ	ZINS
LUX	AXES	FLUX	ROUX	ZIG	FUZZ	RITZ	ZIPS
MAX	AXIL	FOXY	SEXT	ZIN	GAZE	SIZE	ZITI
MIX	AXIS	HOAX	SEXY	ZIP	GEEZ	SIZY	ZITS
NIX	AXLE	IBEX	TAXA	ZIT	HAZE	TZAR	ZOEA
OXO	AXON	ILEX	TAXI	ZOA	HAZY	WHIZ	ZOIC
OXY	BOXY	IXIA	TEXT	ZOO	IZAR	YUTZ	ZONA
PAX	BRUX	JEUX	VEXT	ZUZ	JAZZ	ZAGS	ZONE
PIX	CALX	JINX	WAXY	ZZZ	JEEZ	ZANY	ZONK
POX	COAX	LUXE	XYST	ADZE	LAZE	ZAPS	ZOOM
PYX	COXA	LYNX		AZAN	LAZY	ZARF	ZOON
RAX	CRUX	MAXI	Z	AZON	LUTZ	ZEAL	ZOOS
REX	DEXY	MINX	ZA	BIZE	MAZE	ZEBU	ZORI
SAX	DOUX	MIXT	ADZ	BOZO	MAZY	ZEDS	ZOUK
SEX	DOXY	MOXA	AZO	BUZZ	MEZE	ZEES	ZYME
SIX	EAUX	NEXT	BIZ	CHEZ	MOZO	ZEIN	
SOX	EXAM	NIXE	COZ	COZY	NAZI	ZEKS	

VOWEL-HEAVY WORDS

The following word lists contain all two- through eight-letter words that either consist of many vowels or can help you dispose of multiple I's or U's. The other vowels (A, E, O) generally do not prove problematic because there are a greater number of words containing duplicates of each of these letters. In comparison, while there are no three-letter words containing two I's and only one containing two U's (ULU), there are 12 with two A's, 22 with two E's, and 12 with two O's. Even combinations like GIIIINN may not be so bad if you can dump at least two of the four I's and one of the two N's, leaving GIIN. If an A, D, M, S, or T are available, INIA, NIDI, MINI, NISI, or INTI will do the trick.

Words with 70+% Vowels

AA	AREA	LIEU	ZOEA		
AE	ARIA	LUAU			
AI	ASEA	MEOU	AALII	ABOULIA	EUPNOEA
OE	AURA	MOUE	ADIEU	ACEQUIA	EVACUEE
OI	AWEE	NAOI	AECIA	AECIDIA	EXUVIAE
	BEAU	OBIA	AERIE	AENEOUS	IPOMOEA
EAU	CIAO	OBOE	AIOLI	AEOLIAN	MIAOUED
	EASE	ODEA	AQUAE	AEONIAN	NOUVEAU
AEON	EAUX	OGEE	AREAE	AEROBIA	OIDIOID
AERO	EAVE	OHIA	AUDIO	ALIENEE	OOGONIA
AGEE	EIDE	OLEA	AURAE	AMOEBAE	OUABAIN
AGIO	EMEU	OLEO	AUREI	ANAEMIA	OUGUIYA
AGUE	EPEE	OLIO	COOEE	AQUARIA	ROULEAU
AIDE	ETUI	OOZE	EERIE	AQUEOUS	SEQUOIA
AJEE	EURO	OUZO	LOOIE	AREOLAE	TAENIAE
AKEE	IDEA	QUAI	LOUIE	AUDITEE	URAEMIA
ALAE	ILEA	RAIA	MIAOU	AUREATE	ZOOECIA
ALEE	ILIA	ROUE	OIDIA	AUREOLA	
ALOE	INIA	TOEA	OORIE	AUREOLE	ABOIDEAU
AMIA	IOTA	UNAI	OURIE	AURORAE	ABOITEAU
AMIE	IXIA	UNAU	QUEUE	COUTEAU	AUREOLAE
ANOA	JIAO	UREA	URAEI	EPINAOI	EPOPOEIA
AQUA		UVEA	ZOEAE	EUCAINE	EULOGIAE
				EUGENIA	
				EULOGIA	

BIDI	AIOLI	ICIER	ISSEI	NIHIL	VILLI	SULU	MUCUS
HILI	ALIBI	ICILY	IVIED	NIMBI	VINIC	TUTU	MUMUS
IBIS	AMICI	ICING	IVIES	NISEI	VIRID	ULUS	PUPUS
ILIA	ANIMI	ICTIC	IXIAS	NITID	VISIT	UNAU	QUEUE
IMID	BIALI	IDIOM	JINNI	NIXIE	VIVID	URUS	QUIPU
IMPI	BIDIS	IDIOT	KIBBI	OIDIA	VIZIR		RUBUS
INIA	BIFID	ILIAC	KIBEI	ORIBI	ZITIS	AUGUR	SULUS
INTI	BIKIE	ILIAD	KILIM	PIING	ZIZIT	AURUM	SUNUP
IRID	BINDI	ILIAL	KININ	PIKIS	BIKINI	BUBUS	TUQUE
IRIS	BINIT	ILIUM	KIWIS	PILEI	IMIDIC	BUTUT	TUTUS
IWIS	BLINI	IMIDE	LIBRI	PILIS	IRIDIC	CUTUP	UNAUS
IXIA	CEILI	IMIDO	LICHI	PIPIT	IRITIC	DUFUS	UNCUS
KIWI	CHILI	IMIDS	LICIT	PIXIE	IRITIS	DURUM	UNCUT
LIRI	CILIA	IMINE	LIMBI	PRIMI		FUCUS	UNDUE
MIDI	CIRRI	IMINO	LIMIT	RADII	ULU	FUGUE	USQUE
MINI	CIVIC	IMMIX	LININ	RICIN		FUGUS	USUAL
MIRI	CIVIE	IMPIS	LIPID	RIGID		GURUS	USURP
NIDI	CIVIL	INDIE	LIPIN	RISHI	BUBU	HUMUS	USURY
NISI	DIDIE	INDRI	LITAI	SIGIL	FUGU	JUGUM	UVULA
PIKI	DIGIT	INFIX	LIVID	TEIID	GURU	JUJUS	WUSHU
PILI	DISCI	INION	MEDII	TIBIA	JUJU	JUKUS	
TIKI	DIXIT	INTIS	MIDIS	TIKIS	JUKU	KUDUS	MUUMUU
TIPI	FICIN	IODIC	MILIA	TIMID	KUDU	KUDZU	
TITI	FILMI	IODID	MIMIC	TIPIS	KURU	KURUS	
ZITI	FINIS	IODIN	MINIM	TITIS	LUAU	LUAUS	
AALII	FIXIT	IONIC	MINIS	TORII	LULU	LULUS	
ACINI	GENII	IRIDS	MIRIN	VIGIA	MUMU	LUPUS	
	IAMBI	IRING	MITIS	VIGIL	PUPU	LUSUS	

THE JQXZ NON-BINGO WORD LIST

The best strategy for the high-value letters J, Q, X, and Z is to play them off quickly, usually for 25–35 points, in the hopes of not only scoring well, but of replacing these high-point with low-point value letters, which are more conducive to bingos. Shorter words are generally more likely to be drawn and played than longer words. This is especially true of words containing these four consonants. Also, with these letters, bingo-type scores are possible by playing four- or five-letter words. If you feel you have amply reviewed the short JQXZ plays in the earlier list, focus on the five- and six-letter words below.

J	RAJ	JAUP	JIFF	JOTS	RAJA	JACKY	JAVAS
JO	TAJ	JAVA	JIGS	JOUK	SOJA	JADED	JAWAN
HAJ	AJAR	JAWS	JILL	JOWL	AJIVA	JADES	JAWED
JAB	AJEE	JAYS	JILT	JOWS	AJUGA	JAGER	JAZZY
JAG	DJIN	JAZZ	JIMP	JOYS	BANJO	JAGGS	JEANS
JAM	DOJO	JEAN	JINK	JUBA	BIJOU	JAGGY	JEBEL
JAR	FUJI	JEED	JINN	JUBE	CAJON	JAGRA	JEEPS
JAW	HADJ	JEEP	JINS	JUCO	DJINN	JAILS	JEERS
JAY	HAJI	JEER	JINX	JUDO	DJINS	JAKES	JEFES
JEE	HAJJ	JEES	JIVE	JUGA	DOJOS	JALAP	JEHAD
JET	JABS	JEEZ	JIVY	JUJU	EJECT	JALOP	JEHUS
JEU	JADE	JEFE	JOBS	JUKE	ENJOY	JAMBE	JELLO
JIB	JAGG	JEHU	JOCK	JUKU	FJELD	JAMBS	JELLS
JIG	JAGS	JELL	JOES	JUMP	FJORD	JAMMY	JELLY
JIN	JAIL	JEON	JOEY	JUNK	FUJIS	JANES	JEMMY
JOB	JAKE	JERK	JOGS	JUPE	GANJA	JANTY	JENNY
JOE	JAMB	JESS	JOHN	JURA	HADJI	JAPAN	JERID
JOG	JAMS	JEST	JOIN	JURY	HAJES	JAPED	JERKS
JOT	JANE	JETE	JOKE	JUST	HAJIS	JAPER	JERKY
JOW	JAPE	JETS	JOKY	JUTE	HAJJI	JAPES	JERRY
JOY	JARL	JEUX	JOLE	JUTS	HIJAB	JARLS	JESSE
JUG	JARS	JIAO	JOLT	MOJO	HIJRA	JATOS	JESTS
JUN	JATO	JIBB	JOSH	PUJA	JABOT	JAUKS	JETES
JUS	JAUK	JIBE	JOSS		JACAL	JAUNT	JETON
JUT		JIBS	JOTA		JACKS	JAUPS	JETTY

JEWEL	JUNTO	HAJJES	JEJUNA	JOKERS	JURORS	EQUIP	BARQUE
JIBBS	JUPES	HAJJIS	JEJUNE	JOKIER	JUSTED	FAQIR	BASQUE
JIBED	JUPON	HEJIRA	JELLED	JOKILY	JUSTER	FIQUE	BISQUE
JIBER	JURAL	HIJABS	JELLOS	JOKING	JUSTLE	MAQUI	BOSQUE
JIBES	JURAT	HIJACK	JENNET	JOLTED	JUSTLY	PIQUE	BUQSHA
JIFFS	JUREL	HIJRAH	JERBOA	JOLTER	JUTTED	QADIS	BURQAS
JIFFY	JUROR	HIJRAS	JEREED	JORAMS	KANJIS	QAIDS	CAIQUE
JIGGY	JUSTS	INJECT	JERIDS	JORDAN	KOPJES	QANAT	CALQUE
JIHAD	JUTES	INJURE	JERKED	JORUMS	LOGJAM	QOPHS	CASQUE
JILLS	JUTTY	INJURY	JERKER	JOSEPH	MAJORS	QUACK	CHEQUE
JILTS	KANJI	INKJET	JERKIN	JOSHED	MASJID	QUADS	CINQUE
JIMMY	KOJIS	JABBED	JERRID	JOSHER	MOJOES	QUAFF	CIRQUE
JIMPY	KOPJE	JABBER	JERSEY	JOSHES	MOUJIK	QUAGS	CLAQUE
JINGO	MAJOR	JABIRU	JESSED	JOSSES	MUJIKS	QUAIL	CLIQUE
JINKS	MOJOS	JABOTS	JESSES	JOSTLE	MUSJID	QUAIS	CLIQUY
JINNI	MUJIK	JACALS	JESTED	JOTTED	MUZJIK	QUAKY	CLOQUE
JINNS	NINJA	JACANA	JESTER	JOTTER	NINJAS	QUAKY	COQUET
JIVED	OBJET	JACKAL	JETLAG	JOUALS	OBJECT	QUALE	DIQUAT
JIVER	PUJAH	JACKED	JETONS	JOUKED	OBJETS	QUALM	EQUALS
JIVES	PUJAS	JACKER	JETSAM	JOULES	OUTJUT	QUANT	EQUATE
JIVEY	PUNJI	JACKET	JETSOM	JOUNCE	PAJAMA	QUARE	EQUIDS
JNANA	RAJAH	JADING	JETTED	JOUNCY	PRAJNA	QUARK	EQUINE
JOCKO	RAJAS	JADISH	JETTON	JOURNO	PROJET	QUART	EQUIPS
JOCKS	RAJES	JAEGER	JETWAY	JOUSTS	PUJAHS	QUASH	EQUITY
JOEYS	REJIG	JAGERS	JEWELS	JOVIAL	PUNJIS	QUASI	EXEQUY
JOHNS	RIOJA	JAGGED	JEZAIL	JOWARS	PYJAMA	QUASS	FAQIRS
JOINS	SAJOU	JAGGER	JIBBED	JOWING	RAJAHS	QUATE	FAQUIR
JOINT	SHOJI	JAGRAS	JIBBER	JOWLED	RAMJET	QUAYS	FIQUES
JOIST	SLOJD	JAGUAR	JIBERS	JOYFUL	REJECT	QUBIT	LIQUID
JOKED	SOJAS	JAILED	JIBING	JOYING	REJIGS	QUEAN	LIQUOR
JOKER	TAJES	JAILER	JICAMA	JOYOUS	REJOIN	QUEEN	LOQUAT
JOKES	THUJA	JAILOR	JIGGED	JOYPOP	RIOJAS	QUEER	MANQUE
JOKEY	UNJAM	JALAPS	JIGGER	JUBBAH	ROMAJI	QUELL	MAQUIS
JOLES	ABJECT	JALOPS	JIGGLE	JUBHAH	SAJOUS	QUERN	MARQUE
JOLLY	ABJURE	JALOPY	JIGGLY	JUBILE	SANJAK	QUERY	MASQUE
JOLTS	ACAJOU	JAMBED	JIGSAW	JUDDER	SEJANT	QUEST	MOSQUE
JOLTY	ADJOIN	JAMBES	JIHADS	JUDGED	SHOJIS	QUEUE	OPAQUE
JOMON	ADJURE	JAMMED	JILTED	JUDGER	SLOJDS	QUEYS	PIQUED
JONES	ADJUST	JAMMER	JILTER	JUDGES	SVARAJ	QUICK	PIQUES
JORAM	AJIVAS	JANGLE	JIMINY	JUDOKA	SWARAJ	QUIDS	PIQUET
JORUM	AJOWAN	JANGLY	JIMMIE	JUGATE	THUJAS	QUIET	PLAQUE
JOTAS	AJUGAS	JAPANS	JIMPER	JUGFUL	TRIJET	QUIFF	PULQUE
JOTTY	BANJAX	JAPERS	JIMPLY	JUGGED	UNJAMS	QUILL	QABALA
JOUAL	BANJOS	JAPERY	JINGAL	JUGGLE	UNJUST	QUILT	QANATS
JOUKS	BIJOUS	JAPING	JINGKO	JUGULA	VEEJAY	QUINS	QINDAR
JOULE	BIJOUX	JARFUL	JINGLE	JUGUMS		QUINT	QINTAR
JOUST	BOOJUM	JARGON	JINGLY	JUICED	Q	QUIPS	QIVIUT
JOWAR	CAJOLE	JARINA	JINKED	JUICER	QI	QUIPU	QUACKS
JOWED	COJOIN	JARRAH	JINKER	JUICES	QAT	QUIRE	QUACKY
JOWLS	CROJIK	JARRED	JINNEE	JUJUBE	QIS	QUIRK	QUAERE
JOWLY	DEEJAY	JARVEY	JINNIS	JUKING	QUA	QUIRT	QUAFFS
JOYED	DEJECT	JASMIN	JINXED	JULEPS	SUQ	QUITE	QUAGGA
JUBAS	DJEBEL	JASPER	JINXES	JUMBAL	AQUA	QUITS	QUAGGY
JUBES	DJINNI	JASSID	JITNEY	JUMBLE	QADI	QUODS	QUAHOG
JUCOS	DJINNS	JAUKED	JITTER	JUMBOS	QAID	QUOIN	QUAICH
JUDAS	DJINNY	JAUNCE	JIVERS	JUMPED	QATS	QUOIT	QUAIGH
JUDGE	DONJON	JAUNTS	JIVIER	JUMPER	QOPH	QUOLL	QUAILS
JUDOS	EJECTA	JAUNTY	JIVING	JUNCOS	QUAD	QUOTA	QUAINT
JUGAL	EJECTS	JAUPED	JNANAS	JUNGLE	QUAG	QUOTE	QUAKED
JUGUM	ENJOIN	JAWANS	JOBBED	JUNGLY	QUAI	QUOTH	QUAKER
JUICE	ENJOYS	JAWING	JOBBER	JUNIOR	QUAY	QURSH	QUAKES
JUICY	FAJITA	JAYGEE	JOCKEY	JUNKED	QUEY	ROQUE	QUALIA
JUJUS	FANJET	JAYVEE	JOCKOS	JUNKER	QUID	SQUAB	QUALMS
JUKED	FEIJOA	JAZZBO	JOCOSE	JUNKET	QUIN	SQUAD	QUALMY
JUKES	FJELDS	JAZZED	JOCUND	JUNKIE	QUIP	SQUAT	QUANGO
JUKUS	FJORDS	JAZZER	JOGGED	JUNTAS	QUIT	SQUEG	QUANTA
JULEP	FRIJOL	JAZZES	JOGGER	JUNTOS	QUIZ	SQUIB	QUANTS
JUMBO	GAIJIN	JEANED	JOGGLE	JUPONS	QUOD	SQUID	QUARKS
JUMPS	GANJAH	JEBELS	JOHNNY	JURANT	SUQS	TOQUE	QUARRY
JUMPY	GANJAS	JEEING	JOINED	JURATS	AQUAE	TRANQ	QUARTE
JUNCO	GYTTJA	JEEPED	JOINER	JURELS	AQUAS	TUQUE	QUARTO
JUNKS	HADJEE	JEERED	JOINTS	JURIED	BURQA	UMIAQ	QUARTS
JUNKY	HADJES	JEERER	JOISTS	JURIES	EQUAL	USQUE	QUARTZ
JUNTA	HADJIS	JEHADS	JOJOBA	JURIST	EQUID	ACQUIT	QUASAR

QUATRE	SQUEAL	BRUX	AXMEN	INFIX	SIXTH	BEMIXT	EXILIC
QUAVER	SQUEGS	CALX	AXONE	IXIAS	SIXTY	BIAXAL	EXINES
QUBITS	SQUIBS	COAX	AXONS	IXORA	TAXED	BIFLEX	EXISTS
QUBYTE	SQUIDS	COXA	BEAUX	IXTLE	TAXER	BIJOUX	EXITED
QUEANS	SQUILL	CRUX	BEMIX	KEXES	TAXES	BOLLIX	EXODOI
QUEASY	SQUINT	DEXY	BORAX	KYLIX	TAXIS	BOLLOX	EXODOS
QUEAZY	SQUIRE	DOUX	BOXED	LATEX	TAXOL	BOMBAX	EXODUS
QUEENS	SQUIRM	DOXY	BOXER	LAXER	TAXON	BOMBYX	EXOGEN
QUEERS	SQUIRT	EAUX	BOXES	LAXES	TAXUS	BOXCAR	EXONIC
QUELEA	SQUISH	EXAM	BRAXY	LAXLY	TELEX	BOXERS	EXONYM
QUELLS	SQUUSH	EXEC	BUXOM	LEXES	TEXAS	BOXFUL	EXOTIC
QUENCH	TOQUES	EXED	CALIX	LEXIS	TEXTS	BOXIER	EXPAND
QUERNS	TOQUET	EXES	CALYX	LOXED	TOXIC	BOXILY	EXPATS
QUESTS	TORQUE	EXIT	CAREX	LOXES	TOXIN	BOXING	EXPECT
QUEUED	TRANQS	EXON	CIMEX	LUREX	TUXES	BRUXED	EXPELS
QUEUER	TUQUES	EXPO	CODEX	LUXES	TWIXT	BRUXES	EXPEND
QUEUES	UBIQUE	FALX	COMIX	MAXED	UNBOX	CALXES	EXPERT
QUEZAL	UMIAQS	FAUX	COXAE	MAXES	UNFIX	CAUDEX	EXPIRE
QUICHE	UNIQUE	FIXT	COXAL	MAXIM	UNMIX	CERVIX	EXPIRY
QUICKS	USQUES	FLAX	COXED	MAXIS	UNSEX	CLAXON	EXPORT
QUIETS	YANQUI	FLEX	COXES	MIREX	VARIX	CLIMAX	EXPOSE
QUIFFS		FLUX	CULEX	MIXED	VEXED	COAXAL	EXSECT
QUILLS	X	FOXY	CYLIX	MIXER	VEXER	COAXED	EXSERT
QUILTS	AX	HOAX	DEOXY	MIXES	VEXES	COAXER	EXTANT
QUINCE	EX	IBEX	DESEX	MIXUP	VEXIL	COAXES	EXTEND
QUINIC	OX	ILEX	DETOX	MOXAS	VIXEN	COCCYX	EXTENT
QUININ	XI	IXIA	DEWAX	MOXIE	WAXED	COMMIX	EXTERN
QUINOA	XU	JEUX	DEXES	MUREX	WAXEN	CONVEX	EXTOLL
QUINOL	AXE	JINX	DEXIE	NEXUS	WAXER	CORTEX	EXTOLS
QUINSY	BOX	LUXE	DIXIT	NIXED	WAXES	COWPOX	EXTORT
QUINTA	COX	LYNX	DOXIE	NIXES	XEBEC	COXING	EXTRAS
QUINTE	DEX	MAXI	EPOXY	NIXIE	XENIA	CRUXES	EXUDED
QUINTS	FAX	MINX	EXACT	OXBOW	XENIC	DEIXIS	EXUDES
QUIPPU	FIX	MIXT	EXALT	OXEYE	XENON	DELUXE	EXULTS
QUIPPY	FOX	MOXA	EXAMS	OXIDE	XERIC	DESOXY	EXURBS
QUIPUS	GOX	NEXT	EXCEL	OXIDS	XEROX	DEXIES	EXUVIA
QUIRED	HEX	NIXE	EXECS	OXIME	XERUS	DEXTER	FAXING
QUIRES	KEX	NIXY	EXERT	OXIMS	XYLAN	DEXTRO	FIXATE
QUIRKS	LAX	ONYX	EXILE	OXLIP	XYLEM	DIOXAN	FIXERS
QUIRKY	LEX	ORYX	EXINE	OXTER	XYLOL	DIOXID	FIXING
QUIRTS	LOX	OXEN	EXING	PAXES	XYLYL	DIOXIN	FIXITY
QUITCH	LUX	OXES	EXIST	PHLOX	XYSTI	DIPLEX	FIXURE
QUIVER	MAX	OXID	EXITS	PIXEL	XYSTS	DIXITS	FLAXEN
QUOHOG	MIX	OXIM	EXONS	PIXES	ZAXES	DOXIES	FLAXES
QUOINS	NIX	PIXY	EXPAT	PIXIE	ADIEUX	DUPLEX	FLEXED
QUOITS	OXO	PLEX	EXPEL	POXED	ADMIXT	EARWAX	FLEXES
QUOKKA	OXY	POXY	EXPOS	POXES	ADNEXA	EFFLUX	FLEXOR
QUOLLS	PAX	PREX	EXTOL	PREXY	AFFLUX	ELIXIR	FLUXED
QUORUM	PIX	ROUX	EXTRA	PROXY	ALEXIA	ETHOXY	FLUXES
QUOTAS	POX	SEXT	EXUDE	PYREX	ALEXIN	EUTAXY	FORNIX
QUOTED	PYX	SEXY	EXULT	PYXES	ALKOXY	EXACTA	FOXIER
QUOTER	RAX	TAXA	EXURB	PYXIE	ANNEXE	EXACTS	FOXILY
QUOTES	REX	TAXI	FAXED	PYXIS	ANOXIA	EXALTS	FOXING
QUOTHA	SAX	TEXT	FAXES	RADIX	ANOXIC	EXAMEN	GALAXY
QURUSH	SEX	VEXT	FEDEX	RAXED	APEXES	EXARCH	HALLUX
QWERTY	SIX	WAXY	FIXED	RAXES	ATAXIA	EXCEED	HANDAX
REQUIN	SOX	XYST	FIXER	REDOX	ATAXIC	EXCELS	HATBOX
RISQUE	TAX	ADDAX	FIXES	REDUX	AUSPEX	EXCEPT	HEXADE
ROQUES	TUX	ADMIX	FIXIT	REFIX	AUXINS	EXCESS	HEXADS
ROQUET	VEX	AFFIX	FLAXY	RELAX	AXEMAN	EXCIDE	HEXANE
SACQUE	VOX	ANNEX	FOXED	REMEX	AXEMEN	EXCISE	HEXERS
SEQUEL	WAX	ATAXY	FOXES	REMIX	AXENIC	EXCITE	HEXING
SEQUIN	XIS	AUXIN	GALAX	RETAX	AXILLA	EXCUSE	HEXONE
SHEQEL	ZAX	AXELS	GOXES	REWAX	AXIOMS	EXEDRA	HEXOSE
SQUABS	APEX	AXIAL	HAPAX	REXES	AXIONS	EXEMPT	HEXYLS
SQUADS	AXAL	AXILE	HELIX	SAXES	AXISED	EXEQUY	HOAXED
SQUALL	AXED	AXILS	HEXAD	SEXED	AXISES	EXERTS	HOAXER
SQUAMA	AXEL	AXING	HEXED	SEXES	AXITES	EXEUNT	HOAXES
SQUARE	AXES	AXIOM	HEXER	SEXTO	AXLIKE	EXHALE	HOTBOX
SQUARK	AXIL	AXION	HEXES	SEXTS	AXONAL	EXHORT	IBEXES
SQUASH	AXIS	AXITE	HEXYL	SILEX	AXONES	EXHUME	ICEBOX
SQUATS	AXLE	AXLED	HYRAX	SIXES	AXONIC	EXILED	ILEXES
SQUAWK	AXON	AXLES	IMMIX	SIXMO	AXSEED	EXILER	INFLUX
SQUEAK	BOXY	AXMAN	INDEX	SIXTE	BANJAX	EXILES	IXODID

IXORAS	RAXING	XYLANS	ORZO	BIZES	HERTZ	ZAYIN	BANZAI
IXTLES	REFLEX	XYLEMS	OUZO	BLAZE	HUZZA	ZAZEN	BAZAAR
JINXED	REFLUX	XYLENE	OYEZ	BLITZ	IZARS	ZEALS	BAZARS
JINXES	REMIXT	XYLOID	PHIZ	BONZE	JAZZY	ZEBEC	BAZOOS
KLAXON	REXINE	XYLOLS	PREZ	BOOZE	KANZU	ZEBRA	BEEZER
LARYNX	SAXONY	XYLOSE	PUTZ	BOOZY	KAZOO	ZEBUS	BEGAZE
LAXEST	SCOLEX	XYLYLS	QUIZ	BORTZ	KLUTZ	ZEINS	BENZAL
LAXITY	SEXIER	XYSTER	RAZE	BOZOS	KUDZU	ZERKS	BENZIN
LEXEME	SEXILY	XYSTOI	RAZZ	BRAZA	LAZAR	ZEROS	BENZOL
LEXICA	SEXING	XYSTOS	RITZ	BRAZE	LAZED	ZESTS	BENZYL
LOXING	SEXISM	XYSTUS	SIZE	CAPIZ	LAZES	ZESTY	BEZANT
LUMMOX	SEXIST		SIZY	CLOZE	MAIZE	ZETAS	BEZAZZ
LUXATE	SEXPOT	Z	TZAR	COLZA	MATZA	ZIBET	BEZELS
LUXURY	SEXTAN	ZA	WHIZ	COZEN	MATZO	ZILCH	BEZILS
LYNXES	SEXTET	ADZ	YUTZ	COZES	MAZED	ZILLS	BEZOAR
MASTIX	SEXTON	AZO	ZAGS	COZEY	MAZER	ZINCS	BIZONE
MATRIX	SEXTOS	BIZ	ZANY	COZIE	MAZES	ZINCY	BIZZES
MAXIMA	SEXUAL	COZ	ZAPS	CRAZE	MEZES	ZINEB	BLAZED
MAXIMS	SILVEX	FEZ	ZARF	CRAZY	MEZZO	ZINES	BLAZER
MAXING	SIXMOS	FIZ	ZEAL	CROZE	MIRZA	ZINGS	BLAZES
MAXIXE	SIXTES	WIZ	ZEBU	CZARS	MIZEN	ZINGY	BLAZON
MENINX	SIXTHS	ZAG	ZEDS	DAZED	MOZOS	ZINKY	BLINTZ
MINXES	SKYBOX	ZAP	ZEES	DAZES	MUZZY	ZIPPY	BLOWZY
MIXERS	SMILAX	ZAS	ZEIN	DIAZO	NAZIS	ZIRAM	BONZER
MIXING	SPADIX	ZAX	ZEKS	DITZY	NERTZ	ZITIS	BONZES
MIXUPS	SPHINX	ZED	ZEPS	DIZEN	NIZAM	ZIZIT	BOOZED
MOXIES	SPHYNX	ZEE	ZERK	DIZZY	NUDZH	ZLOTE	BOOZER
MUSKOX	STORAX	ZEK	ZERO	DOOZY	OOZED	ZLOTY	BOOZES
MYXOID	STYRAX	ZEP	ZEST	DOZED	OOZES	ZOEAE	BORZOI
MYXOMA	SUBFIX	ZIG	ZETA	DOZEN	ORZOS	ZOEAL	BRAIZE
NIXIES	SUFFIX	ZIN	ZIGS	DOZER	OUZEL	ZOEAS	BRAZAS
NIXING	SURTAX	ZIP	ZILL	DOZES	OUZOS	ZOMBI	BRAZED
NONTAX	SYNTAX	ZIT	ZINC	ENZYM	OZONE	ZONAE	BRAZEN
ONYXES	SYRINX	ZOA	ZINE	FAZED	PIZZA	ZONAL	BRAZER
ORYXES	TAXEME	ZOO	ZING	FAZES	PLAZA	ZONED	BRAZES
OUTBOX	TAXERS	ZUZ	ZINS	FEAZE	PLOTZ	ZONER	BRAZIL
OUTFOX	TAXIED	ZZZ	ZIPS	FEEZE	PRIZE	ZONES	BREEZE
OXALIC	TAXIES	ADZE	ZITI	FEZES	RAZED	ZONKS	BREEZY
OXALIS	TAXING	AZAN	ZITS	FEZZY	RAZEE	ZOOEY	BRONZE
OXBOWS	TAXITE	AZON	ZOEA	FIZZY	RAZER	ZOOID	BRONZY
OXCART	TAXMAN	BIZE	ZOIC	FRITZ	RAZES	ZOOKS	BUZUKI
OXEYES	TAXMEN	BOZO	ZONA	FRIZZ	RAZOR	ZOOMS	BUZZED
OXFORD	TAXOLS	BUZZ	ZONE	FROZE	RITZY	ZOONS	BUZZER
OXIDES	TAXONS	CHEZ	ZONK	FURZE	SCUZZ	ZOOTY	BUZZES
OXIDIC	TEABOX	COZY	ZOOM	FURZY	SEIZE	ZORIL	BYZANT
OXIMES	THORAX	CZAR	ZOON	FUZED	SIZAR	ZORIS	CHAZAN
OXLIKE	TOXICS	DAZE	ZOOS	FUZEE	SIZED	ZOUKS	CHINTZ
OXLIPS	TOXINE	DITZ	ZORI	FUZES	SIZER	ZOWIE	CLOZES
OXTAIL	TOXINS	DOZE	ZOUK	FUZIL	SIZES	ZUZIM	COLZAS
OXTERS	TOXOID	DOZY	ZYME	FUZZY	SMAZE	ZYMES	CORYZA
OXYGEN	TUXEDO	FAZE	ABUZZ	GAUZE	SOYUZ	ABLAZE	COZENS
PAXWAX	UNAXED	FIZZ	ADOZE	GAUZY	SOZIN	ADZING	COZEYS
PEGBOX	UNFIXT	FOZY	ADZED	GAZAR	SPITZ	ADZUKI	COZIED
PEROXY	UNISEX	FRIZ	ADZES	GAZED	TAZZA	AGNIZE	COZIER
PHENIX	UNMIXT	FUTZ	AGAZE	GAZER	TAZZE	AMAZED	COZIES
PICKAX	UNSEXY	FUZE	AMAZE	GAZES	TIZZY	AMAZES	COZILY
PIXELS	UNVEXT	FUZZ	AZANS	GHAZI	TOPAZ	AMAZON	COZZES
PIXIES	URTEXT	GAZE	AZIDE	GIZMO	TROOZ	ASSIZE	CRAZED
PLEXAL	VERNIX	GEEZ	AZIDO	GLAZE	TZARS	AZALEA	CRAZES
PLEXES	VERTEX	HAZE	AZINE	GLAZY	UNZIP	AZIDES	CROZER
PLEXOR	VEXERS	HAZY	AZLON	GLITZ	VIZIR	AZINES	CROZES
PLEXUS	VEXILS	IZAR	AZOIC	GLOZE	VIZOR	AZLONS	DAZING
POLEAX	VEXING	JAZZ	AZOLE	GONZO	WALTZ	AZOLES	DAZZLE
POLLEX	VIXENS	JEEZ	AZONS	GRAZE	WHIZZ	AZONAL	DEFUZE
POXIER	VOLVOX	LAZE	AZOTE	GROSZ	WINZE	AZONIC	DEZINC
POXING	VORTEX	LAZY	AZOTH	GYOZA	WIZEN	AZOTED	DIAZIN
PRAXES	WAXERS	LUTZ	AZUKI	HAFIZ	WIZES	AZOTES	DITZES
PRAXIS	WAXIER	MAZE	AZURE	HAMZA	WOOZY	AZOTHS	DIZENS
PREFIX	WAXILY	MAZY	BAIZA	HAZAN	ZAIRE	AZOTIC	DIZZES
PREMIX	WAXING	MEZE	BAIZE	HAZED	ZAMIA	AZUKIS	DONZEL
PRETAX	XEBECS	MOZO	BAZAR	HAZEL	ZANZA	AZURES	DOOZER
PREXES	XENIAL	NAZI	BAZOO	HAZER	ZAPPY	AZYGOS	DOOZIE
PROLIX	XENIAS	OOZE	BEZEL	HAZES	ZARFS	BAIZAS	DOZENS
PYXIES	XENONS	OOZY	BEZIL	HEEZE	ZAXES	BAIZES	DOZIER

136

DOZILY	GAUZES	IZZARD	MIRZAS	PUZZLE	SOZINS	ZANANA	ZIRCON
DOZING	GAZABO	JAZZBO	MIZENS	QUARTZ	SPELTZ	ZANDER	ZITHER
ECZEMA	GAZARS	JAZZED	MIZUNA	QUEAZY	SPRITZ	ZANIER	ZIZITH
ENZYME	GAZEBO	JAZZER	MIZZEN	QUEZAL	STANZA	ZANIES	ZIZZLE
ENZYMS	GAZERS	JAZZES	MIZZLE	RAZEED	SYZYGY	ZANILY	ZLOTYS
EPIZOA	GAZING	JEZAIL	MIZZLY	RAZEES	TARZAN	ZANZAS	ZOARIA
ERSATZ	GAZUMP	KANZUS	MOMZER	RAZERS	TAZZAS	ZAPPED	ZOCALO
EVZONE	GEEZER	KAZOOS	MUZHIK	RAZING	TEAZEL	ZAPPER	ZODIAC
FAZING	GHAZIS	KHAZEN	MUZJIK	RAZORS	TEAZLE	ZAREBA	ZOECIA
FEAZED	GIZMOS	KIBITZ	MUZZLE	RAZZED	TOUZLE	ZARIBA	ZOFTIG
FEAZES	GLAZED	KLUTZY	NAZIFY	RAZZES	TWEEZE	ZAYINS	ZOMBIE
FEEZED	GLAZER	KOLHOZ	NIZAMS	REBOZO	TZETZE	ZAZENS	ZOMBIS
FEEZES	GLAZES	KOLKOZ	NOZZLE	RESIZE	TZURIS	ZEALOT	ZONARY
FEZZED	GLITZY	KUDZUS	NUZZLE	REZERO	UNZIPS	ZEATIN	ZONATE
FIZGIG	GLOZED	KUVASZ	OOZIER	REZONE	UPGAZE	ZEBECK	ZONERS
FIZZED	GLOZES	KWANZA	OOZILY	RITZES	UPSIZE	ZEBECS	ZONING
FIZZER	GRAZED	LAZARS	OOZING	ROZZER	VIZARD	ZEBRAS	ZONKED
FIZZES	GRAZER	LAZIED	OUZELS	SCHIZO	VIZIER	ZECHIN	ZONULA
FIZZLE	GRAZES	LAZIER	OYEZES	SCHIZY	VIZIRS	ZENANA	ZONULE
FLOOZY	GROSZE	LAZIES	OZALID	SCHNOZ	VIZORS	ZENITH	ZOOIDS
FOOZLE	GROSZY	LAZILY	OZONES	SCUZZY	VIZSLA	ZEPHYR	ZOOIER
FOZIER	GUZZLE	LAZING	OZONIC	SEIZED	WHEEZE	ZEROED	ZOOMED
FRAZIL	GYOZAS	LAZULI	PANZER	SEIZER	WHEEZY	ZEROES	ZOONAL
FREEZE	HALUTZ	LIZARD	PATZER	SEIZES	WHIZZY	ZEROTH	ZOONED
FRENZY	HAMZAH	LUTZES	PAZAZZ	SEIZIN	WINZES	ZESTED	ZORILS
FRIEZE	HAMZAS	MAHZOR	PHIZES	SEIZOR	WIZARD	ZESTER	ZOSTER
FRIZED	HAZANS	MAIZES	PIAZZA	SHAZAM	WIZENS	ZEUGMA	ZOUAVE
FRIZER	HAZARD	MAMZER	PIAZZE	SIZARS	WIZZEN	ZIBETH	ZOUNDS
FRIZES	HAZELS	MATZAH	PIZAZZ	SIZERS	WIZZES	ZIBETS	ZOYSIA
FRIZZY	HAZERS	MATZAS	PIZZAS	SIZIER	WURZEL	ZIGGED	ZYDECO
FROUZY	HAZIER	MATZOH	PIZZAZ	SIZING	YAKUZA	ZIGZAG	ZYGOID
FROWZY	HAZILY	MATZOS	PIZZLE	SIZZLE	YUTZES	ZILLAH	ZYGOMA
FROZEN	HAZING	MATZOT	PLAZAS	SLEAZE	ZADDIK	ZINCED	ZYGOSE
FURZES	HAZMAT	MAZARD	PODZOL	SLEAZO	ZAFFAR	ZINCIC	ZYGOTE
FUTZED	HAZZAN	MAZERS	POTZER	SLEAZY	ZAFFER	ZINCKY	ZYMASE
FUTZES	HEEZED	MAZIER	POZOLE	SMAZES	ZAFFIR	ZINEBS	
FUZEES	HEEZES	MAZILY	PREZES	SNAZZY	ZAFFRE	ZINGED	
FUZILS	HUTZPA	MAZING	PRIZED	SNEEZE	ZAFTIG	ZINGER	
FUZING	HUZZAH	MAZUMA	PRIZER	SNEEZY	ZAGGED	ZINNIA	
FUZZED	HUZZAS	MEZCAL	PRIZES	SNOOZE	ZAIKAI	ZIPPED	
FUZZES	IODIZE	MEZZOS	PUTZED	SNOOZY	ZAIRES	ZIPPER	
	IONIZE	MEZUZA	PUTZES	SOZINE	ZAMIAS	ZIRAMS	

FOUR-LETTER WORDS

Informal research of Scrabble games between experts indicates that 75 percent of all words formed in a game are short words—words of two, three, or four letters. In addition, these words account for 50 percent of all points scored. With short words comprising only 5 percent of the dictionary, their contribution to the game is disproportionately great. It also suggests that word-studiers will get a much greater payoff by judiciously selecting the shorter words to learn. Another part of the payoff is learning the root words to longer words, including bonus plays. DRAY can be extended into DRAYING, MAZY can become MAZIEST, while TINT is the root of TINTERS. Studying the 101 two-letter words and 1004 three-letter words is no small accomplishment. So how do you approach 4002 four-letter words? Grab a highlighter and mark those words that you (a) do not know, (b) might consider challenging if played by your opponent, or (c) feel you may have difficulty seeing within a group of seven random letters. At your leisure, review only your highlighted words.

AAHS	ABET	ABYS	ACME	ADDS	AERY	AGER	AGMA
AALS	ABLE	ACED	ACNE	ADIT	AFAR	AGES	AGOG
ABAS	ABLY	ACES	ACRE	ADOS	AGAR	AGHA	AGON
ABBA	ABRI	ACHE	ACTA	ADZE	AGAS	AGIN	AGUE
ABBE	ABUT	ACHY	ACTS	AEON	AGED	AGIO	AHED
ABED	ABYE	ACID	ACYL	AERO	AGEE	AGLY	AHEM

AHIS	ANTS	BABA	BERG	BOIL	BULB	CARP	CLOD
AHOY	ANUS	BABE	BERK	BOLA	BULK	CARR	CLOG
AIDE	APED	BABU	BERM	BOLD	BULL	CARS	CLON
AIDS	APER	BABY	BEST	BOLE	BUMF	CART	CLOP
AILS	APES	BACH	BETA	BOLO	BUMP	CASA	CLOT
AIMS	APEX	BACK	BETH	BOLT	BUMS	CASE	CLOY
AINS	APOD	BADE	BETS	BOMB	BUNA	CASH	CLUB
AIRN	APOS	BADS	BEVY	BOND	BUND	CASK	CLUE
AIRS	APPS	BAFF	BEYS	BONE	BUNG	CAST	COAL
AIRT	APSE	BAGS	BHUT	BONG	BUNK	CATE	COAT
AIRY	AQUA	BAHT	BIAS	BONK	BUNN	CATS	COAX
AITS	ARAK	BAIL	BIBB	BONY	BUNS	CAUL	COBB
AJAR	ARBS	BAIT	BIBS	BOOB	BUNT	CAVE	COBS
AJEE	ARCH	BAKE	BICE	BOOK	BUOY	CAVY	COCA
AKEE	ARCO	BALD	BIDE	BOOM	BURA	CAWS	COCK
AKIN	ARCS	BALE	BIDI	BOON	BURB	CAYS	COCO
ALAE	AREA	BALK	BIDS	BOOR	BURD	CECA	CODA
ALAN	ARES	BALL	BIER	BOOS	BURG	CEDE	CODE
ALAR	ARFS	BALM	BIFF	BOOT	BURL	CEDI	CODS
ALAS	ARIA	BALS	BIGS	BOPS	BURN	CEES	COED
ALBA	ARID	BAMS	BIKE	BORA	BURP	CEIL	COFF
ALBS	ARIL	BAND	BILE	BORE	BURR	CELL	COFT
ALEC	ARKS	BANE	BILK	BORK	BURS	CELS	COGS
ALEE	ARMS	BANG	BILL	BORN	BURY	CELT	COHO
ALEF	ARMY	BANI	BIMA	BORT	BUSH	CENT	COIF
ALES	ARTS	BANK	BIND	BOSH	BUSK	CEPE	COIL
ALFA	ARTY	BANS	BINE	BOSK	BUSS	CEPS	COIN
ALGA	ARUM	BAPS	BINS	BOSS	BUST	CERE	COIR
ALIF	ARVO	BARB	BINT	BOTA	BUSY	CERO	COKE
ALIT	ARYL	BARD	BIOG	BOTH	BUTE	CESS	COKY
ALKY	ASCI	BARE	BIOS	BOTS	BUTS	CETE	COLA
ALLS	ASEA	BARF	BIRD	BOTT	BUTT	CHAD	COLD
ALLY	ASHY	BARK	BIRK	BOUT	BUYS	CHAI	COLE
ALMA	ASKS	BARM	BIRL	BOWL	BUZZ	CHAM	COLS
ALME	ASPS	BARN	BIRO	BOWS	BYES	CHAO	COLT
ALMS	ATAP	BARS	BIRR	BOXY	BYRE	CHAP	COLY
ALOE	ATES	BASE	BISE	BOYO	BYRL	CHAR	COMA
ALOW	ATMA	BASH	BISK	BOYS	BYTE	CHAT	COMB
ALPS	ATOM	BASK	BITE	BOZO	CABS	CHAW	COME
ALSO	ATOP	BASS	BITS	BRAD	CACA	CHAY	COMP
ALTO	AUKS	BAST	BITT	BRAE	CADE	CHEF	CONE
ALTS	AULD	BATE	BIZE	BRAG	CADI	CHEW	CONI
ALUM	AUNT	BATH	BLAB	BRAN	CADS	CHEZ	CONK
AMAH	AURA	BATS	BLAE	BRAS	CAFE	CHIA	CONN
AMAS	AUTO	BATT	BLAH	BRAT	CAFF	CHIC	CONS
AMBO	AVER	BAUD	BLAM	BRAW	CAGE	CHID	CONY
AMEN	AVES	BAWD	BLAT	BRAY	CAGY	CHIN	COOF
AMIA	AVID	BAWL	BLAW	BRED	CAID	CHIP	COOK
AMID	AVOS	BAYS	BLEB	BREE	CAIN	CHIS	COOL
AMIE	AVOW	BEAD	BLED	BREN	CAKE	CHIT	COON
AMIN	AWAY	BEAK	BLET	BREW	CAKY	CHON	COOP
AMIR	AWED	BEAM	BLEW	BRIE	CALF	CHOP	COOS
AMIS	AWEE	BEAN	BLIN	BRIG	CALK	CHOW	COOT
AMMO	AWES	BEAR	BLIP	BRIM	CALL	CHUB	COPE
AMOK	AWLS	BEAT	BLOB	BRIN	CALM	CHUG	COPS
AMPS	AWNS	BEAU	BLOC	BRIO	CALO	CHUM	COPY
AMUS	AWNY	BECK	BLOG	BRIS	CALX	CIAO	CORD
AMYL	AWOL	BEDS	BLOT	BRIT	CAME	CIGS	CORE
ANAL	AWRY	BEDU	BLOW	BROO	CAMO	CINE	CORF
ANAS	AXAL	BEEF	BLUB	BROS	CAMP	CION	CORK
ANDS	AXED	BEEN	BLUE	BROW	CAMS	CIRE	CORM
ANES	AXEL	BEEP	BLUR	BRRR	CANE	CIST	CORN
ANEW	AXES	BEER	BOAR	BRUT	CANS	CITE	CORS
ANGA	AXIL	BEES	BOAS	BRUX	CANT	CITY	CORY
ANIL	AXIS	BEET	BOAT	BUBO	CAPE	CLAD	COSH
ANIS	AXLE	BEGS	BOBS	BUBS	CAPH	CLAG	COSS
ANKH	AXON	BELL	BOCK	BUBU	CAPO	CLAM	COST
ANNA	AYAH	BELS	BODE	BUCK	CAPS	CLAN	COSY
ANOA	AYES	BELT	BODS	BUDS	CARB	CLAP	COTE
ANON	AYIN	BEMA	BODY	BUFF	CARD	CLAW	COTS
ANSA	AZAN	BEND	BOFF	BUGS	CARE	CLAY	COUP
ANTA	AZON	BENE	BOGS	BUHL	CARK	CLEF	COVE
ANTE	BAAL	BENS	BOGY	BUHR	CARL	CLEW	COWL
ANTI	BAAS	BENT	BOHO		CARN	CLIP	COWS

COWY	DARB	DIFF	DOUR	EASY	ETIC	FEMS	FOAL
COXA	DARE	DIFS	DOUX	EATH	ETNA	FEND	FOAM
COYS	DARK	DIGS	DOVE	EATS	ETUI	FENS	FOBS
COZY	DARN	DIKE	DOWN	EAUX	EURO	FEOD	FOCI
CRAB	DART	DILL	DOWS	EAVE	EVEN	FERE	FOES
CRAG	DASH	DIME	DOXY	EBBS	EVER	FERN	FOGS
CRAM	DATA	DIMS	DOZE	EBON	EVES	FESS	FOGY
CRAP	DATE	DINE	DOZY	ECHE	EVIL	FEST	FOHN
CRAW	DATO	DING	DRAB	ECHO	EWER	FETA	FOIL
CRED	DAUB	DINK	DRAG	ECHT	EWES	FETE	FOIN
CREW	DAUT	DINO	DRAM	ECRU	EXAM	FETS	FOLD
CRIB	DAVY	DINS	DRAT	ECUS	EXEC	FEUD	FOLK
CRIS	DAWK	DINT	DRAW	EDDO	EXED	FEUS	FOND
CRIT	DAWN	DIOL	DRAY	EDDY	EXES	FIAR	FONS
CROC	DAWS	DIPS	DREE	EDGE	EXIT	FIAT	FONT
CROP	DAWT	DIPT	DREG	EDGY	EXON	FIBS	FOOD
CROW	DAYS	DIRE	DREK	EDHS	EXPO	FICE	FOOL
CRUD	DAZE	DIRK	DREW	EDIT	EYAS	FICO	FOOT
CRUS	DEAD	DIRL	DRIB	EELS	EYED	FIDO	FOPS
CRUX	DEAF	DIRT	DRIP	EELY	EYEN	FIDS	FORA
CUBE	DEAL	DISC	DROP	EERY	EYER	FIEF	FORB
CUBS	DEAN	DISH	DRUB	EFFS	EYES	FIFE	FORD
CUDS	DEAR	DISK	DRUG	EFTS	EYNE	FIGS	FORE
CUED	DEBS	DISS	DRUM	EGAD	EYRA	FILA	FORK
CUES	DEBT	DITA	DRYS	EGAL	EYRE	FILE	FORM
CUFF	DECK	DITE	DUAD	EGER	EYRY	FILL	FORT
CUIF	DECO	DITS	DUAL	EGGS	FABS	FILM	FOSS
CUKE	DEED	DITZ	DUBS	EGGY	FACE	FILO	FOUL
CULL	DEEM	DIVA	DUCE	EGIS	FACT	FILS	FOUR
CULM	DEEP	DIVE	DUCI	EGOS	FADE	FIND	FOWL
CULT	DEER	DJIN	DUCK	EIDE	FADO	FINE	FOXY
CUPS	DEES	DOAT	DUCT	EKED	FADS	FINK	FOYS
CURB	DEET	DOBY	DUDE	EKES	FAGS	FINO	FOZY
CURD	DEFI	DOCK	DUDS	ELAN	FAIL	FINS	FRAE
CURE	DEFT	DOCS	DUEL	ELDS	FAIN	FIRE	FRAG
CURF	DEFY	DODO	DUES	ELHI	FAIR	FIRM	FRAP
CURL	DEIL	DOER	DUET	ELKS	FAKE	FIRN	FRAT
CURN	DEKE	DOES	DUFF	ELLS	FALL	FIRS	FRAY
CURR	DELE	DOFF	DUGS	ELMS	FALX	FISC	FREE
CURS	DELF	DOGE	DUIT	ELMY	FAME	FISH	FRET
CURT	DELI	DOGS	DUKE	ELSE	FANE	FIST	FRIG
CUSK	DELL	DOGY	DULL	EMES	FANG	FITS	FRIT
CUSP	DELS	DOIT	DULY	EMEU	FANO	FIVE	FRIZ
CUSS	DELT	DOJO	DUMA	EMIC	FANS	FIXT	FROE
CUTE	DEME	DOLE	DUMB	EMIR	FARD	FIZZ	FROG
CUTS	DEMO	DOLL	DUMP	EMIT	FARE	FLAB	FROM
CWMS	DEMY	DOLS	DUNE	EMMY	FARL	FLAG	FROW
CYAN	DENE	DOLT	DUNG	EMUS	FARM	FLAK	FRUG
CYMA	DENI	DOME	DUNK	EMYD	FARO	FLAM	FUBS
CYME	DENS	DOMS	DUNS	ENDS	FASH	FLAN	FUCI
CYST	DENT	DONA	DUNT	ENGS	FAST	FLAP	FUDS
CZAR	DENY	DONE	DUOS	ENOL	FATE	FLAT	FUEL
DABS	DERE	DONG	DUPE	ENOW	FATS	FLAW	FUGS
DACE	DERM	DONS	DUPS	ENUF	FAUN	FLAX	FUGU
DADA	DESK	DOOM	DURA	ENVY	FAUX	FLAY	FUJI
DADO	DEVA	DOOR	DURE	EONS	FAVA	FLEA	FULL
DADS	DEVS	DOPA	DURN	EPEE	FAVE	FLED	FUME
DAFF	DEWS	DOPE	DURO	EPHA	FAWN	FLEE	FUMY
DAFT	DEWY	DOPY	DURR	EPIC	FAYS	FLEW	FUND
DAGS	DEXY	DORE	DUSK	EPOS	FAZE	FLEX	FUNK
DAHL	DEYS	DORK	DUST	ERAS	FEAL	FLEY	FUNS
DAHS	DHAK	DORM	DUTY	ERGO	FEAR	FLIC	FURL
DAIS	DHAL	DORP	DYAD	ERGS	FEAT	FLIP	FURS
DAKS	DHOW	DORR	DYED	ERNE	FECK	FLIR	FURY
DALE	DIAL	DORS	DYER	ERNS	FEDS	FLIT	FUSE
DALS	DIBS	DORY	DYES	EROS	FEEB	FLOC	FUSS
DAME	DICE	DOSE	DYKE	ERRS	FEED	FLOE	FUTZ
DAMN	DICK	DOSS	DYNE	ERST	FEEL	FLOG	FUZE
DAMP	DIDO	DOST	EACH	ESES	FEES	FLOP	FUZZ
DAMS	DIDY	DOTE	EARL	ESNE	FEET	FLOW	FYCE
DANG	DIED	DOTH	EARN	ESPY	FEHS	FLUB	FYKE
DANK	DIEL	DOTS	EARS	ETAS	FELL	FLUE	GABS
DANS	DIES	DOTY	EASE	ETCH	FELT	FLUS	GABY
DAPS	DIET	DOUM	EAST	ETHS	FEME	FLUX	GADI

139

GADS	GILD	GRAY	HANG	HIPS	HURT	JAGS	JUKU
GAED	GILL	GREE	HANK	HIRE	HUSH	JAIL	JUMP
GAEN	GILT	GREW	HANT	HISN	HUSK	JAKE	JUNK
GAES	GIMP	GREY	HAPS	HISS	HUTS	JAMB	JUPE
GAFF	GINK	GRID	HARD	HIST	HWAN	JAMS	JURA
GAGA	GINS	GRIG	HARE	HITS	HYLA	JANE	JURY
GAGE	GIPS	GRIM	HARK	HIVE	HYMN	JAPE	JUST
GAGS	GIRD	GRIN	HARL	HOAR	HYPE	JARL	JUTE
GAIN	GIRL	GRIP	HARM	HOAX	HYPO	JARS	JUTS
GAIT	GIRN	GRIT	HARP	HOBO	HYPS	JATO	KAAS
GALA	GIRO	GROG	HART	HOBS	HYTE	JAUK	KABS
GALE	GIRT	GROK	HASH	HOCK	IAMB	JAUP	KADI
GALL	GIST	GROT	HASP	HODS	IBEX	JAVA	KAES
GALS	GITE	GROW	HAST	HOED	IBIS	JAWS	KAFS
GAMA	GITS	GRUB	HATE	HOER	ICED	JAYS	KAGU
GAMB	GIVE	GRUE	HATH	HOES	ICES	JAZZ	KAIF
GAME	GLAD	GRUM	HATS	HOGG	ICHS	JEAN	KAIL
GAMP	GLAM	GUAN	HAUL	HOGS	ICKY	JEED	KAIN
GAMS	GLED	GUAR	HAUT	HOKE	ICON	JEEP	KAKA
GAMY	GLEE	GUCK	HAVE	HOLD	IDEA	JEER	KAKI
GANE	GLEG	GUDE	HAWK	HOLE	IDEM	JEES	KALE
GANG	GLEN	GUFF	HAWS	HOLK	IDES	JEEZ	KAME
GAOL	GLEY	GUID	HAYS	HOLM	IDLE	JEFE	KAMI
GAPE	GLIA	GULF	HAZE	HOLP	IDLY	JEHU	KANA
GAPS	GLIB	GULL	HAZY	HOLS	IDOL	JELL	KANE
GAPY	GLIM	GULP	HEAD	HOLT	IDYL	JEON	KAON
GARB	GLOB	GULS	HEAL	HOLY	IFFY	JERK	KAPA
GARS	GLOM	GUMS	HEAP	HOME	IGGS	JESS	KAPH
GASH	GLOP	GUNK	HEAR	HOMO	IGLU	JEST	KARN
GASP	GLOW	GUNS	HEAT	HOMY	IKAT	JETE	KART
GAST	GLUE	GURU	HECK	HONE	IKON	JETS	KATA
GATE	GLUG	GUSH	HEED	HONG	ILEA	JEUX	KATS
GATS	GLUM	GUST	HEEL	HONK	ILEX	JIAO	KAVA
GAUD	GLUT	GUTS	HEFT	HONS	ILIA	JIBB	KAYO
GAUM	GNAR	GUVS	HEHS	HOOD	ILKA	JIBE	KAYS
GAUN	GNAT	GUYS	HEIL	HOOF	ILKS	JIBS	KBAR
GAUR	GNAW	GYBE	HEIR	HOOK	ILLS	JIFF	KEAS
GAVE	GNUS	GYMS	HELD	HOOP	ILLY	JIGS	KECK
GAWK	GOAD	GYPS	HELL	HOOT	IMAM	JILL	KEEF
GAWP	GOAL	GYRE	HELM	HOPE	IMID	JILT	KEEK
GAYS	GOAS	GYRI	HELO	HOPS	IMMY	JIMP	KEEL
GAZE	GOAT	GYRO	HELP	HORA	IMPI	JINK	KEEN
GEAR	GOBO	GYVE	HEME	HORN	IMPS	JINN	KEEP
GECK	GOBS	HAAF	HEMP	HOSE	INBY	JINS	KEET
GEDS	GOBY	HAAR	HEMS	HOST	INCH	JINX	KEFS
GEED	GODS	HABU	HENS	HOTS	INFO	JIVE	KEGS
GEEK	GOER	HACK	HENT	HOUR	INIA	JIVY	KEIR
GEES	GOES	HADE	HERB	HOVE	INKS	JOBS	KELP
GEEZ	GOGO	HADJ	HERD	HOWE	INKY	JOCK	KELT
GELD	GOLD	HAED	HERE	HOWF	INLY	JOES	KEMP
GELS	GOLF	HAEM	HERL	HOWK	INNS	JOEY	KENO
GELT	GONE	HAEN	HERM	HOWL	INRO	JOGS	KENS
GEMS	GONG	HAES	HERN	HOWS	INTI	JOHN	KENT
GENE	GOOD	HAET	HERO	HOYA	INTO	JOIN	KEPI
GENS	GOOF	HAFT	HERS	HOYS	IONS	JOKE	KEPS
GENT	GOOK	HAGS	HEST	HUBS	IOTA	JOKY	KEPT
GENU	GOON	HAHA	HETH	HUCK	IRED	JOLE	KERB
GERM	GOOP	HAHS	HETS	HUED	IRES	JOLT	KERF
GEST	GOOS	HAIK	HEWN	HUES	IRID	JOSH	KERN
GETA	GORE	HAIL	HEWS	HUFF	IRIS	JOSS	KETO
GETS	GORM	HAIR	HICK	HUGE	IRKS	JOTA	KEYS
GEUM	GORP	HAJI	HIDE	HUGS	IRON	JOTS	KHAF
GHAT	GORY	HAJJ	HIED	HUIC	ISBA	JOUK	KHAN
GHEE	GOSH	HAKE	HIES	HULA	ISLE	JOWL	KHAT
GHIS	GOTH	HAKU	HIGH	HULK	ISMS	JOWS	KHET
GIBE	GOUT	HALE	HIKE	HULL	ITCH	JOYS	KHIS
GIBS	GOWD	HALF	HILA	HUMP	ITEM	JUBA	KIBE
GIDS	GOWK	HALL	HILI	HUMS	IWIS	JUBE	KICK
GIED	GOWN	HALM	HILL	HUNG	IXIA	JUCO	KIDS
GIEN	GRAB	HALO	HILT	HUNH	IZAR	JUDO	KIEF
GIES	GRAD	HALT	HIMS	HUNK	JABS	JUGA	KIER
GIFT	GRAM	HAME	HIND	HUNS	JACK	JUGS	KIFS
GIGA	GRAN	HAMS	HINS	HUNT	JADE	JUJU	KILL
GIGS	GRAT	HAND	HINT	HURL	JAGG	JUKE	KILN

KILO	LAID	LIBS	LOOS	MAKE	MEWS	MOOS	NARY
KILT	LAIN	LICE	LOOT	MAKO	MEZE	MOOT	NAVE
KINA	LAIR	LICH	LOPE	MALE	MHOS	MOPE	NAVY
KIND	LAKE	LICK	LOPS	MALL	MIBS	MOPS	NAYS
KINE	LAKH	LIDO	LORD	MALM	MICA	MOPY	NAZI
KING	LAKY	LIDS	LORE	MALT	MICE	MORA	NEAP
KINK	LALL	LIED	LORN	MAMA	MICS	MORE	NEAR
KINO	LAMA	LIEF	LORY	MANA	MIDI	MORN	NEAT
KINS	LAMB	LIEN	LOSE	MANE	MIDS	MORS	NEBS
KIPS	LAME	LIER	LOSS	MANO	MIEN	MORT	NECK
KIRK	LAMP	LIES	LOST	MANS	MIFF	MOSH	NEED
KIRN	LAMS	LIEU	LOTA	MANY	MIGG	MOSK	NEEM
KIRS	LAND	LIFE	LOTH	MAPS	MIGS	MOSS	NEEP
KISS	LANE	LIFT	LOTI	MARA	MIKE	MOST	NEGS
KIST	LANG	LIKE	LOTS	MARC	MILD	MOTE	NEIF
KITE	LANK	LILO	LOUD	MARE	MILE	MOTH	NEMA
KITH	LAPS	LILT	LOUP	MARK	MILK	MOTS	NENE
KITS	LARD	LILY	LOUR	MARL	MILL	MOTT	NEON
KIVA	LARI	LIMA	LOUT	MARS	MILO	MOUE	NERD
KIWI	LARK	LIMB	LOVE	MART	MILS	MOVE	NESS
KLIK	LARS	LIME	LOWE	MASA	MILT	MOWN	NEST
KNAP	LASE	LIMN	LOWN	MASH	MIME	MOWS	NETS
KNAR	LASH	LIMO	LOWS	MASK	MINA	MOXA	NETT
KNEE	LASS	LIMP	LUAU	MASS	MIND	MOZO	NEUK
KNEW	LAST	LIMY	LUBE	MAST	MINE	MUCH	NEUM
KNIT	LATE	LINE	LUCE	MATE	MINI	MUCK	NEVE
KNOB	LATH	LING	LUCK	MATH	MINK	MUDS	NEVI
KNOP	LATI	LINK	LUDE	MATS	MINT	MUFF	NEWS
KNOT	LATS	LINN	LUES	MATT	MINX	MUGG	NEWT
KNOW	LATU	LINO	LUFF	MAUD	MIPS	MUGS	NEXT
KNUR	LAUD	LINS	LUGE	MAUL	MIRE	MULE	NIBS
KOAN	LAVA	LINT	LUGS	MAUN	MIRI	MULL	NICE
KOAS	LAVE	LINY	LULL	MAUT	MIRK	MUMM	NICK
KOBO	LAVS	LION	LULU	MAWN	MIRS	MUMP	NIDE
KOBS	LAWN	LIPA	LUMA	MAWS	MIRY	MUMS	NIDI
KOEL	LAWS	LIPE	LUMP	MAXI	MISE	MUMU	NIGH
KOHL	LAYS	LIPS	LUMS	MAYA	MISO	MUNI	NILL
KOIS	LAZE	LIRA	LUNA	MAYO	MISS	MUNS	NILS
KOJI	LAZY	LIRE	LUNE	MAYS	MIST	MUON	NIMS
KOLA	LEAD	LIRI	LUNG	MAZE	MITE	MURA	NINE
KOLO	LEAF	LISP	LUNK	MAZY	MITT	MURE	NIPA
KONK	LEAK	LIST	LUNT	MEAD	MITY	MURK	NIPS
KOOK	LEAL	LITE	LUNY	MEAL	MIXT	MURR	NISI
KOPH	LEAN	LITS	LURE	MEAN	MOAN	MUSE	NITE
KOPS	LEAP	LITU	LURK	MEAT	MOAS	MUSH	NITS
KORA	LEAR	LIVE	LUSH	MEDS	MOAT	MUSK	NIXE
KORE	LEAS	LOAD	LUST	MEED	MOBS	MUSS	NIXY
KORS	LECH	LOAF	LUTE	MEEK	MOCK	MUST	NOBS
KOSS	LEEK	LOAM	LUTZ	MEET	MOCS	MUTE	NOCK
KOTO	LEER	LOAN	LUVS	MEGA	MODE	MUTS	NODE
KRIS	LEES	LOBE	LUXE	MEGS	MODI	MUTT	NODI
KUDO	LEET	LOBO	LWEI	MELD	MODS	MYCS	NODS
KUDU	LEFT	LOBS	LYCH	MELL	MOGS	MYNA	NOEL
KUES	LEGS	LOCA	LYES	MELS	MOIL	MYTH	NOES
KUFI	LEHR	LOCH	LYNX	MELT	MOJO	NAAN	NOGG
KUNA	LEIS	LOCI	LYRE	MEME	MOKE	NABE	NOGS
KUNE	LEKE	LOCK	LYSE	MEMO	MOLA	NABS	NOIL
KURU	LEKS	LOCO	MAAR	MEMS	MOLD	NADA	NOIR
KVAS	LEKU	LODE	MABE	MEND	MOLE	NAFF	NOLO
KYAK	LEND	LOFT	MACE	MENO	MOLL	NAGS	NOMA
KYAR	LENO	LOGE	MACH	MENU	MOLS	NAIF	NOME
KYAT	LENS	LOGO	MACK	MEOU	MOLT	NAIL	NOMS
KYES	LENT	LOGS	MACS	MEOW	MOLY	NALA	NONA
KYTE	LEPT	LOGY	MADE	MERC	MOME	NAME	NONE
LABS	LESS	LOID	MADS	MERE	MOMI	NANA	NOOK
LACE	LEST	LOIN	MAES	MERK	MOMS	NANS	NOON
LACK	LETS	LOLL	MAGE	MERL	MONK	NAOI	NOPE
LACS	LEUD	LONE	MAGI	MESA	MONO	NAOS	NORI
LACY	LEVA	LONG	MAGS	MESH	MONS	NAPA	NORM
LADE	LEVO	LOOF	MAID	MESS	MONY	NAPE	NOSE
LADS	LEVY	LOOK	MAIL	META	MOOD	NAPS	NOSH
LADY	LEWD	LOOM	MAIM	METE	MOOL	NARC	NOSY
LAGS	LEYS	LOON	MAIN	METH	MOON	NARD	NOTA
LAIC	LIAR	LOOP	MAIR	MEWL	MOOR	NARK	NOTE

NOUN	OOZE	PANS	PIAL	PONE	PUPS	RAWS	ROAD
NOUS	OOZY	PANT	PIAN	PONG	PUPU	RAYA	ROAM
NOVA	OPAH	PAPA	PIAS	PONS	PURE	RAYS	ROAN
NOWS	OPAL	PAPS	PICA	PONY	PURI	RAZE	ROAR
NOWT	OPED	PARA	PICE	POOD	PURL	RAZZ	ROBE
NUBS	OPEN	PARD	PICK	POOF	PURR	READ	ROBS
NUDE	OPES	PARE	PICS	POOH	PURS	REAL	ROCK
NUKE	OPTS	PARK	PIED	POOL	PUSH	REAM	ROCS
NULL	OPUS	PARR	PIER	POON	PUSS	REAP	RODE
NUMB	ORAD	PARS	PIES	POOP	PUTS	REAR	RODS
NUNS	ORAL	PART	PIGS	POOR	PUTT	REBS	ROES
NURD	ORBS	PASE	PIKA	POPE	PUTZ	RECK	ROIL
NURL	ORBY	PASH	PIKE	POPS	PYAS	RECS	ROLE
NUTS	ORCA	PASS	PIKI	PORE	PYES	REDD	ROLF
OAFS	ORCS	PAST	PILE	PORK	PYIC	REDE	ROLL
OAKS	ORDO	PATE	PILI	PORN	PYIN	REDO	ROMP
OAKY	ORES	PATH	PILL	PORT	PYRE	REDS	ROMS
OARS	ORGY	PATS	PILY	POSE	PYRO	REED	ROOD
OAST	ORLE	PATY	PIMA	POSH	QADI	REEF	ROOF
OATH	ORRA	PAVE	PIMP	POST	QAID	REEK	ROOK
OATS	ORTS	PAWL	PINA	POSY	QATS	REEL	ROOM
OBAS	ORYX	PAWN	PINE	POTS	QOPH	REES	ROOT
OBES	ORZO	PAWS	PING	POUF	QUAD	REFS	ROPE
OBEY	OSAR	PAYS	PINK	POUR	QUAG	REFT	ROPY
OBIA	OSES	PEAG	PINS	POUT	QUAI	REGS	ROSE
OBIS	OSSA	PEAK	PINT	POWS	QUAY	REIF	ROSY
OBIT	OTIC	PEAL	PINY	POXY	QUEY	REIN	ROTA
OBOE	OTTO	PEAN	PION	PRAM	QUID	REIS	ROTE
OBOL	OUCH	PEAR	PIPE	PRAO	QUIN	RELY	ROTI
OCAS	OUDS	PEAS	PIPS	PRAT	QUIP	REMS	ROTL
ODAH	OUPH	PEAT	PIPY	PRAU	QUIT	REND	ROTO
ODAS	OURS	PECH	PIRN	PRAY	QUIZ	RENT	ROTS
ODDS	OUST	PECK	PISH	PREE	QUOD	REPO	ROUE
ODEA	OUTS	PECS	PISO	PREP	RACE	REPP	ROUP
ODES	OUZO	PEDS	PITA	PREX	RACK	REPS	ROUT
ODIC	OVAL	PEEK	PITH	PREY	RACY	RESH	ROUX
ODOR	OVEN	PEEL	PITS	PREZ	RADS	REST	ROVE
ODYL	OVER	PEEN	PITY	PRIG	RAFF	RETE	ROWS
OFFS	OVUM	PEEP	PIXY	PRIM	RAFT	RETS	RUBE
OGAM	OWED	PEER	PLAN	PROA	RAGA	REVS	RUBS
OGEE	OWES	PEES	PLAT	PROD	RAGE	RHEA	RUBY
OGLE	OWLS	PEGS	PLAY	PROF	RAGG	RHOS	RUCK
OGRE	OWNS	PEHS	PLEA	PROG	RAGI	RHUS	RUDD
OHED	OWSE	PEIN	PLEB	PROM	RAGS	RIAL	RUDE
OHIA	OXEN	PEKE	PLED	PROP	RAIA	RIAS	RUED
OHMS	OXES	PELE	PLEW	PROS	RAID	RIBS	RUER
OILS	OXID	PELF	PLEX	PROW	RAIL	RICE	RUES
OILY	OXIM	PELT	PLIE	PSIS	RAIN	RICH	RUFF
OINK	OYER	PEND	PLOD	PSST	RAIS	RICK	RUGA
OKAS	OYES	PENS	PLOP	PTUI	RAJA	RIDE	RUGS
OKAY	OYEZ	PENT	PLOT	PUBS	RAKE	RIDS	RUIN
OKEH	PACA	PEON	PLOW	PUCE	RAKI	RIEL	RULE
OKES	PACE	PEPO	PLOY	PUCK	RAKU	RIFE	RULY
OKRA	PACK	PEPS	PLUG	PUDS	RALE	RIFF	RUMP
OLDS	PACS	PERE	PLUM	PUFF	RAMI	RIFS	RUMS
OLDY	PACT	PERI	PLUS	PUGH	RAMP	RIFT	RUNE
OLEA	PACY	PERK	POCK	PUGS	RAMS	RIGS	RUNG
OLEO	PADI	PERM	POCO	PUJA	RAND	RILE	RUNS
OLES	PADS	PERP	PODS	PUKE	RANG	RILL	RUNT
OLIO	PAGE	PERT	POEM	PULA	RANI	RIME	RUSE
OLLA	PAID	PERV	POET	PULE	RANK	RIMS	RUSH
OMEN	PAIK	PESO	POGY	PULI	RANT	RIMY	RUSK
OMER	PAIL	PEST	POIS	PULL	RAPE	RIND	RUST
OMIT	PAIN	PETS	POKE	PULP	RAPS	RING	RUTH
ONCE	PAIR	PEWS	POKY	PULS	RAPT	RINK	RUTS
ONES	PALE	PFFT	POLE	PUMA	RARE	RINS	RYAS
ONLY	PALL	PFUI	POLL	PUMP	RASE	RIOT	RYES
ONOS	PALM	PHAT	POLO	PUNA	RASH	RIPE	RYKE
ONTO	PALP	PHEW	POLS	PUNG	RASP	RIPS	RYND
ONUS	PALS	PHIS	POLY	PUNK	RATE	RISE	RYOT
ONYX	PALY	PHIZ	POME	PUNS	RATH	RISK	SABE
OOHS	PAMS	PHON	POMO	PUNT	RATO	RITE	SABS
OOPS	PANE	PHOT	POMP	PUNY	RATS	RITZ	SACK
OOTS	PANG	PHUT	POND	PUPA	RAVE	RIVE	SACS

142

SADE	SELS	SIRS	SOFT	STOT	TALE	THIS	TORE
SADI	SEME	SITE	SOIL	STOW	TALI	THOU	TORI
SAFE	SEMI	SITH	SOJA	STUB	TALK	THRO	TORN
SAGA	SEND	SITS	SOKE	STUD	TALL	THRU	TORO
SAGE	SENE	SIZE	SOLA	STUM	TAME	THUD	TORR
SAGO	SENT	SIZY	SOLD	STUN	TAMP	THUG	TORS
SAGS	SEPT	SKAG	SOLE	STYE	TAMS	THUS	TORT
SAGY	SERA	SKAS	SOLI	SUBA	TANG	TICK	TORY
SAID	SERE	SKAT	SOLO	SUBS	TANK	TICS	TOSH
SAIL	SERF	SKEE	SOLS	SUCH	TANS	TIDE	TOSS
SAIN	SERS	SKEG	SOMA	SUCK	TAOS	TIDY	TOST
SAKE	SETA	SKEP	SOME	SUDD	TAPA	TIED	TOTE
SAKI	SETS	SKEW	SOMS	SUDS	TAPE	TIER	TOTS
SALE	SETT	SKID	SONE	SUED	TAPS	TIES	TOUR
SALL	SEWN	SKIM	SONG	SUER	TARE	TIFF	TOUT
SALP	SEWS	SKIN	SONS	SUES	TARN	TIKE	TOWN
SALS	SEXT	SKIP	SOOK	SUET	TARO	TIKI	TOWS
SALT	SEXY	SKIS	SOON	SUGH	TARP	TILE	TOWY
SAME	SHAD	SKIT	SOOT	SUIT	TARS	TILL	TOYO
SAMP	SHAG	SKUA	SOPH	SUKS	TART	TILS	TOYS
SAND	SHAH	SLAB	SOPS	SULK	TASK	TILT	TRAD
SANE	SHAM	SLAG	SORA	SULU	TASS	TIME	TRAM
SANG	SHAW	SLAM	SORB	SUMO	TATE	TINE	TRAP
SANK	SHAY	SLAP	SORD	SUMP	TATS	TING	TRAY
SANS	SHEA	SLAT	SORE	SUMS	TAUS	TINS	TREE
SAPS	SHED	SLAW	SORI	SUNG	TAUT	TINT	TREF
SARD	SHES	SLAY	SORN	SUNK	TAVS	TINY	TREK
SARI	SHEW	SLED	SORT	SUNN	TAWS	TIPI	TRES
SARK	SHIM	SLEW	SOTH	SUNS	TAXA	TIPS	TRET
SASH	SHIN	SLID	SOTS	SUPE	TAXI	TIRE	TREY
SASS	SHIP	SLIM	SOUK	SUPS	TEAK	TIRL	TRIG
SATE	SHIV	SLIP	SOUL	SUQS	TEAL	TIRO	TRIM
SATI	SHMO	SLIT	SOUP	SURA	TEAM	TITI	TRIO
SAUL	SHOD	SLOB	SOUR	SURD	TEAR	TITS	TRIP
SAVE	SHOE	SLOE	SOUS	SURE	TEAS	TIVY	TROD
SAWN	SHOG	SLOG	SOWN	SURF	TEAT	TOAD	TROG
SAWS	SHOO	SLOP	SOWS	SUSS	TECH	TOBY	TROP
SAYS	SHOP	SLOT	SOYA	SWAB	TEDS	TODS	TROT
SCAB	SHOT	SLOW	SOYS	SWAG	TEED	TODY	TROW
SCAD	SHOW	SLUB	SPAE	SWAM	TEEL	TOEA	TROY
SCAG	SHRI	SLUE	SPAM	SWAN	TEEM	TOED	TRUE
SCAM	SHUL	SLUG	SPAN	SWAP	TEEN	TOES	TRUG
SCAN	SHUN	SLUM	SPAR	SWAT	TEES	TOFF	TSAR
SCAR	SHUT	SLUR	SPAS	SWAY	TEFF	TOFT	TSKS
SCAT	SHWA	SLUT	SPAT	SWIG	TEGG	TOFU	TUBA
SCOP	SIAL	SMEW	SPAY	SWIM	TEGS	TOGA	TUBE
SCOT	SIBB	SMIT	SPEC	SWOB	TELA	TOGS	TUBS
SCOW	SIBS	SMOG	SPED	SWOP	TELE	TOIL	TUCK
SCRY	SICE	SMUG	SPEW	SWOT	TELL	TOIT	TUFA
SCUD	SICK	SMUT	SPIN	SWUM	TELS	TOKE	TUFF
SCUM	SICS	SNAG	SPIT	SYBO	TEMP	TOLA	TUFT
SCUP	SIDE	SNAP	SPIV	SYCE	TEND	TOLD	TUGS
SCUT	SIDH	SNAW	SPOT	SYKE	TENS	TOLE	TUIS
SEAL	SIFT	SNED	SPRY	SYLI	TENT	TOLL	TULE
SEAM	SIGH	SNIB	SPUD	SYNC	TEPA	TOLU	TUMP
SEAR	SIGN	SNIP	SPUE	SYNE	TERM	TOMB	TUNA
SEAS	SIKA	SNIT	SPUN	SYPH	TERN	TOME	TUNE
SEAT	SIKE	SNOB	SPUR	TABS	TEST	TOMS	TUNG
SECS	SILD	SNOG	SRIS	TABU	TETH	TONE	TUNS
SECT	SILK	SNOT	STAB	TACE	TETS	TONG	TUPS
SEED	SILL	SNOW	STAG	TACH	TEWS	TONS	TURF
SEEK	SILO	SNUB	STAR	TACK	TEXT	TONY	TURK
SEEL	SILT	SNUG	STAT	TACO	THAE	TOOK	TURN
SEEM	SIMA	SNYE	STAW	TACT	THAN	TOOL	TUSH
SEEN	SIMP	SOAK	STAY	TADS	THAT	TOOM	TUSK
SEEP	SIMS	SOAP	STEM	TAEL	THAW	TOON	TUTS
SEER	SINE	SOAR	STEP	TAGS	THEE	TOOT	TUTU
SEES	SING	SOBA	STET	TAHR	THEM	TOPE	TWAE
SEGO	SINH	SOBS	STEW	TAIL	THEN	TOPH	TWAS
SEGS	SINK	SOCA	STEY	TAIN	THEW	TOPI	TWEE
SEIF	SINS	SOCK	STIR	TAKA	THEY	TOPO	TWIG
SEIS	SIPE	SODA	STOA	TAKE	THIN	TOPS	TWIN
SELF	SIPS	SODS	STOB	TALA	THIO	TORA	TWIT
SELL	SIRE	SOFA	STOP	TALC	THIR	TORC	TWOS

143

TYEE	UTES	VIGA	WANT	WERT	WITH	YARN	YUCA
TYER	UVEA	VIGS	WANY	WEST	WITS	YAUD	YUCH
TYES	VACS	VILE	WAPS	WETS	WIVE	YAUP	YUCK
TYIN	VAGI	VILL	WARD	WHAM	WOAD	YAWL	YUGA
TYKE	VAIL	VIMS	WARE	WHAP	WOES	YAWN	YUKS
TYNE	VAIN	VINA	WARK	WHAT	WOKE	YAWP	YULE
TYPE	VAIR	VINE	WARM	WHEE	WOKS	YAWS	YUPS
TYPO	VALE	VINO	WARN	WHEN	WOLD	YAYS	YURT
TYPP	VAMP	VINY	WARP	WHET	WOLF	YEAH	YUTZ
TYPY	VANE	VIOL	WARS	WHEW	WOMB	YEAN	YWIS
TYRE	VANG	VIRL	WART	WHEY	WONK	YEAR	ZAGS
TYRO	VANS	VISA	WARY	WHID	WONS	YEAS	ZANY
TZAR	VARA	VISE	WASH	WHIG	WONT	YECH	ZAPS
UDON	VARS	VITA	WASP	WHIM	WOOD	YEGG	ZARF
UDOS	VARY	VIVA	WAST	WHIN	WOOF	YELD	ZEAL
UGHS	VASA	VIVE	WATS	WHIP	WOOL	YELK	ZEBU
UGLY	VASE	VOES	WATT	WHIR	WOOS	YELL	ZEDS
UKES	VAST	VOID	WAUK	WHIT	WORD	YELP	ZEES
ULAN	VATS	VOLE	WAUL	WHIZ	WORE	YENS	ZEIN
ULNA	VATU	VOLT	WAUR	WHOA	WORK	YEPS	ZEKS
ULUS	VAUS	VOTE	WAVE	WHOM	WORM	YERK	ZEPS
ULVA	VAVS	VOWS	WAVY	WHOP	WORN	YETI	ZERK
UMBO	VAWS	VROW	WAWL	WHUP	WORT	YETT	ZERO
UMPS	VEAL	VUGG	WAWS	WHYS	WOST	YEUK	ZEST
UNAI	VEEP	VUGH	WAXY	WICH	WOTS	YEWS	ZETA
UNAU	VEER	VUGS	WAYS	WICK	WOVE	YILL	ZIGS
UNBE	VEES	WABS	WEAK	WIDE	WOWS	YINS	ZILL
UNCI	VEIL	WACK	WEAL	WIFE	WRAP	YIPE	ZINC
UNCO	VEIN	WADE	WEAN	WIGS	WREN	YIPS	ZINE
UNDE	VELA	WADI	WEAR	WILD	WRIT	YIRD	ZING
UNDO	VELD	WADS	WEBS	WILE	WUSS	YIRR	ZINS
UNDY	VENA	WADY	WEDS	WILL	WYCH	YLEM	ZIPS
UNIT	VEND	WAES	WEED	WILT	WYES	YOBS	ZITI
UNTO	VENT	WAFF	WEEK	WILY	WYLE	YOCK	ZITS
UPAS	VERA	WAFT	WEEL	WIMP	WYND	YODH	ZOEA
UPBY	VERB	WAGE	WEEN	WIND	WYNN	YODS	ZOIC
UPDO	VERT	WAGS	WEEP	WINE	WYNS	YOGA	ZONA
UPON	VERY	WAIF	WEER	WING	WYTE	YOGH	ZONE
URBS	VEST	WAIL	WEES	WINK	XYST	YOGI	ZONK
URDS	VETO	WAIN	WEET	WINO	YACK	YOKE	ZOOM
UREA	VETS	WAIR	WEFT	WINS	YAFF	YOKS	ZOON
URGE	VEXT	WAIT	WEIR	WINY	YAGI	YOLK	ZOOS
URIC	VIAL	WAKE	WEKA	WIPE	YAGS	YOND	ZORI
URNS	VIBE	WALE	WELD	WIRE	YAKS	YONI	ZOUK
URPS	VICE	WALK	WELL	WIRY	YALD	YORE	ZYME
URSA	VIDE	WALL	WELT	WISE	YAMS	YOUR	
URUS	VIDS	WALY	WEND	WISH	YANG	YOUS	
USED	VIED	WAME	WENS	WISP	YANK	YOWE	
USER	VIER	WAND	WENT	WISS	YAPS	YOWL	
USES	VIES	WANE	WEPT	WIST	YARD	YOWS	
UTAS	VIEW	WANS	WERE	WITE	YARE	YUAN	